D1447658

DIY MEDIATION

DIY MEDIATION

The Conflict Resolution Toolkit for HR

Marc Reid

Matador
9 Priory Business Park,
Wistow Road, Kibworth Beauchamp,
Leicestershire. LE8 0RX
Tel: 0116 279 2299
Email: books@troubador.co.uk
Web: www.troubador.co.uk/matador
Twitter: @matadorbooks

ISBN 978 1785893 117

British Library Cataloguing in Publication Data.
A catalogue record for this book is available from the British Library.

Printed and bound in the UK by TJ International, Padstow, Cornwall
Typeset in 11pt Aldine401 BT by Troubador Publishing Ltd, Leicester, UK

Matador is an imprint of Troubador Publishing Ltd

Contents

Foreword   ix
Acknowledgements   xi

1. Introduction   xiii

2. The Issue (what you should know) – Part 1   1

    Introduction   3
    What is Conflict?   3
        - Negative vs Positive   3
        - Is it a Conflict?   5
        - Conflict Ingredients   6
    Recognising Conflict   9
        - Activity Indicators   10
        - Behavioural Indicators   11
    How Conflict Evolves   14
    Options for Dealing with Conflict   16
        - Three Conflict Resolution Options   16
        - Roadmap for Appropriate Intervention   18

2. The Issue (what is useful to know) – Part 2   29

    Conflict Issues   31
    Needs and the Conflict Iceberg   34
    Why Does it Matter?   36
        - Cost of Conflict – Direct Costs   38
        - Cost of Conflict – Intangibles   42
    Stages of Conflict Escalation   43
    Different Styles of Conflict Response   47
        - Five Conflict Styles   49
        - Adapting Conflict Styles   51

3. The Skills   55

    Introduction   57
    Questioning   57
        - Open Questions   57
        - Closed Questions   60
        - Hypothetical Questions   60
        - Questioning Pitfalls   62
        - Planning Your Questions   63
    Active Listening   64
        - Reflecting   66
        - Enquiring   66
        - Acknowledging   67
        - Summarising   68
        - Silence   69
        - Unspoken Communication   69
        - Rephrasing   72
        - Encouraging   72
        - Barriers to Active Listening   73
    Assertive Communication   77
    Impartiality   82

4. The Process   89

    Introduction   91
    Background to the AGREE Model   91
    Phase 1 – Act   96
        - Preparation   96
        - Opening the Individual Meeting   99
    Phase 2 – Gather Information   102
        - Establishing Needs and Interests   105
        - Closing the Individual Meeting   106
    Phase 3 – Recognise Issues   109
        - Joint Meeting – Preparation   109

CONTENTS

- Joint Meeting – Opening 110
- Joint Meeting – Individual Time 111
- Joint Meeting – Discussion Opening 113
- Joint Meeting – Addressing the Trigger Point 114
- Joint Meeting – Dealing with Emotion 115
- Joint Meeting – Handling a Demand for
  an Apology 116
- Joint Meeting – Summarising Issues 118

Phase 4 – Explore Solutions 120
- Joint Meeting – Brainstorm Issues 120
- Joint Meeting – Looking for Conciliatory
  Gestures 122
- Joint Meeting – Reality Testing 123
- Joint Meeting – Identify Mutually Agreeable
  Solutions for Each Issue 124
- Joint Meeting – Agreeing a Mechanism for
  Dealing with Future Issues 125
- Joint Meeting – Dealing with Blockages 125

Phase 5 – Encourage Agreement 130
- Joint Meeting – Writing the Agreement 130
- Joint Meeting – What to Include in the
  Agreement 132
- Joint Meeting – Agreement Confidentiality 133
- Joint Meeting – Closing 133
- Follow Up 134

Using AGREE for Difficult Conversations 135
- Difficult Conversations – Preparation 136
- Difficult Conversations – Meeting Process 142

Dealing with Challenging Behaviour 143
- Challenging People 145

5. And Finally... 151
- Five Top Strategies for Conflict
  Competence 154

6. Quick Reference   159

7. Appendices   181
    1. Barb and Sue Case Study   183
    2. Barb and Sue Agreement   197
    3. AGREE Model Summary   199
    4. Sample Questions   200
    5. Simple Conflict Styles Questionnaire   203
    6. Access to Further Resources   207

Foreword

During my twenty years of experience working as a Human Resources professional, I have observed that human relationships within the working environment are often the baseline for the success or failure of a particular team, department or organisation. Forming and maintaining relationships can be challenging at the best of times, but within the work environment where employees are faced with the pressure of targets, deadlines and the requirement to work as part of a team, things are even more complicated.

As line managers or HR specialists our natural position is to assume that people will 'get on', and it is not until a particular incident flares up that we realise this is a very simplistic view. Understanding human behaviour, particularly in the area of conflict, allows us to take a more informed and deliberate approach to human interaction at work.

In writing this book, Marc Reid has drawn on his broad experience as a line manager, HR specialist and most recently mediator to provide us with both a robust insight into the academic theory pertaining to conflict, as well as offering a practical step-by-step guide of how to identify, assess and resolve conflict.

For most of us conflict resolution is not an area that we feel particularly confident or comfortable with. However, this book is written with that in mind and uses a range of methods, including case studies, models and flow charts, to help the reader build up their capability and confidence.

From my own experience I fully support Marc's view that having some basic knowledge about conflict and a simple framework to address it will help the reader not only to deal with current situations that need to be resolved but more importantly prevent future disagreements or differences of opinion escalating into full-blown conflicts.

For me this book is a valuable resource which I will keep in my office library to be consulted on a frequent basis, not only when conflict appears, but also as a healthy reminder that employees as human beings have emotional needs which must be considered on a regular basis and should not be pushed into the background when other business priorities emerge.

Martha Desmond
Chief Human Resources Officer, Apollo Tyres

Acknowledgements

My thanks go to all those who have encouraged and supported me in the writing of this book. In particular I am grateful to George and Tracey at BBB who helped me take that initial step of putting pen to paper (or typing the first letter in Word!), and to Teak Rehman whose excellent coaching kept me on course during the writing. Thank you to the clients I have trained and to those I have mediated. The experience I have gained in working with them has been invaluable in helping me develop and refine my thinking for the book. I am grateful to Martha, an outstanding HR Director whom I respect enormously, for sparing time to read the book and say such kind words in the Foreword. Finally, a massive thank you to my family for their encouragement, especially my wife, Kathy, who has provided inspiration, challenge, insight and never-ending motivation.

Section 1
Introduction

What this book is about

Conflict is an inescapable element of every workplace. Most of the time it is minor – a disagreement over how to address a problem, a misunderstanding on what was wanted, some feedback that is poorly communicated. In nearly all these situations the people involved will sort it out themselves and that will be the end of it. Where HR comes into it is when it is not sorted. The people with the issue and their line manager have not been able to nip it in the bud and it lands on your desk as an employee relations issue to resolve.

So what do you do? Of course you can reach for your policies and procedures folder to pull out the company grievance policy. How many of those day-to-day relationship issues though can really be sorted with the formal process? You could try mediation. Do you really need at this stage to bring someone else in to mediate? It's a relatively low-level issue at the moment. After all, if you were rewiring your house you'd call in an electrician, but to change a lightbulb or replace a plug you'd do it yourself, wouldn't you? But you would still need to know what you were doing. If you put the wrong wire in the wrong terminal you could end up with a serious situation.

This is how DIY Mediation came about. Having worked as a professional mediator and previously in HR, I know that there are many HR professionals out there who could be capable of dealing with low-level conflict. Yet they haven't been given the guidance or framework – a roadmap of what you need and how to do it, just as you have to know what tools you need and which wire goes where when rewiring a plug. That's what this book is about. It is not about training you to be a professional mediator. It is about giving you the necessary know-how and framework to use a mediation-style approach to nip low-level conflict in the bud.

I've taken the essence of what I have learned as a mediator and turned it into a pragmatic approach, combining a set of critical skills and a simple process that can be easily picked up and put into practice quickly. The emphasis in this book is very much on practical application. I've therefore given you lots of tools that can be useful in applying DIY Mediation. If you are looking for theoretical or academic complexity then you are likely to be disappointed. I've touched on some theory but only to the extent that it adds to your practical understanding and makes you more effective in using DIY Mediation. Should you want the more in-depth, full mediator's manual complete with theory there are other books out there for you. However, if you are someone who wants to grow their toolbox with practical options to support line managers and employees, then DIY Mediation is the right book for you.

Why I wrote this book

I put together the AGREE model which forms the basis for the DIY Mediation approach some years ago and have been training HR and line managers in its use ever since. I had never intended to start training others but often in my mediation work I saw conflict escalate as opportunities were missed for it to be nipped in the bud. The competence and confidence were lacking to make the necessary timely intervention. That is when I put together the model and developed the training. The feedback has been excellent. Participants in the workshop really value the simple approach and feel it is something they can usefully apply in the workplace. The next step was to try to spread the message wider and a book was the obvious choice. I was always reluctant to say I was training people in 'mediation' because to do full mediation training takes a lot longer than the workshops I was running. When I needed a name for the book therefore I came up with DIY Mediation as that fits with the approach I am advocating. It takes the essence of mediation but makes it simple and pragmatic such that people can use it as part of their day-to-day job – literally a 'do it yourself' approach.

Who can use DIY Mediation?

DIY Mediation is primarily intended for use by HR professionals. You might be an HR manager with responsibility for supporting the line or an HR consultant providing support to smaller companies. It is straightforward enough for line managers to use themselves but the focus in this book is on providing a conflict resolution toolkit for the HR professional. For DIY Mediation to work, you should follow the process and apply the skills. This won't necessarily result in a resolution to the conflict between the participants – in the end it is their responsibility to find a solution. But it gives you an approach that if used correctly gives the participants every possibility to resolve their issues. Most people can follow a process but the more challenging part is the skills. In Section 3 I cover the key skills you will need. The extent to which you can develop these skills will be the primary factor in determining your success.

The DIY Mediation approach is based on you acting as an impartial facilitator, helping the participants in the conflict find a way forward themselves. Having now trained hundreds of people in this approach and seen them try it out through role play, it is clear that some are simply not comfortable with this style. This is not surprising. We have been trained over many years as line and HR to 'sort things out'. So standing back and facilitating is a different approach that takes time to get used to. It takes practice – some people will pick it up fairly easily, others realise it is simply not for them and will look to other options. This could be asking someone who is confident in this approach to help them or considering the other options available. In Section 2 Part 1 we look at what other options are open to HR and the manager alongside DIY Mediation.

When should you use DIY Mediation?

The general rule of thumb is that the earlier a problem can be addressed the more chance you have of resolving it. The vast majority of conflicts that arise will be resolved by the individuals themselves. However, if they can't resolve it, more often than not the first port of call will be the line manager – or the observant line manager may notice that something is amiss before any of the individuals alert them to it. Once the issue has been flagged the manager will need to decide their response. Section 2 Part 1 introduces you to the Roadmap for Appropriate Intervention, which gives options on dealing with conflict at different stages. This is a useful guide but ultimately it is normally down to you and / or the manager to decide when the individuals are not going to resolve it themselves. At that point an intervention is needed. The attraction of using an informal approach such as DIY Mediation is that it can be set up very quickly and doesn't involve anyone else, thereby preventing the kind of escalation that a formal process would entail.

As a guide, therefore, here are five questions to help you decide if it is time to use DIY Mediation. If the answer to most of these is 'yes' then it is probably appropriate:

- Have the individuals tried to resolve it themselves but are not able to do so?
- Is the issue causing the conflict non-binary i.e. there is not a simple yes / no or right / wrong?
- If not addressed could the issue escalate and cause further damage?

- Is there no simple solution that could be implemented which would fully resolve the issue?
- Do you feel sufficiently competent and confident to start the process?

Most conflicts end up being serious as they have not been addressed early enough. This is often because the person responsible for addressing it has either not recognised the issue or has recognised it and avoided dealing with it. An avoiding strategy may be appropriate if you have decided this is the most appropriate option. However, simply ignoring the problem and hoping it will go away is inevitably going to lead to conflict escalation and more problems down the line. To summarise, intervene earlier rather than later so you can nip conflict in the bud and avoid additional problems for yourself, the organisation and more pain for the people involved.

How to use this book

There are three main sections to this book which I've titled The Issue, The Skills and The Process. Throughout I give examples to demonstrate practical application and many of these refer to a case study which runs through the book. If, once you've read the book, you want a rapid reminder of the key points there is a quick reference section at the end which gives you the key messages in double-quick time.

In The Issue section I give you an understanding of conflict. I know what it is like working in a busy HR environment; you'll have little time to spare, so I've split the section into two – what you should know and what is useful to know. If you are really desperate to get on with the nuts and bolts of DIY Mediation you can always skip Part 2 and instead jump ahead to The Skills. Part 1 looks at what conflict is, what indicates there could be conflict and options for tackling it. Part 2 explores conflict in more depth, looks at why it is important we deal with it and considers how people respond to conflict differently.

The Skills section takes you through what I consider to be the four key skills you need when using DIY Mediation. These are Questioning, Active Listening, Assertive Communication and Impartiality. I'll show you what the important elements are of these skills and provide several helpful tools to make applying the skills that much easier.

The section on The Process introduces you to the AGREE model and takes you through the five phases in detail. Each phase includes guidance on what to look out for and tips on how to tackle the likely situations you will experience. I take you through the meeting structure within which you apply the model and will show you how the model can be applied when you are not helping others resolve an issue but you are part of the conflict or potential conflict yourself – what we think of as 'difficult conversations'. I'll look at generic types of difficult behaviour and finish up with my top five strategies for being a truly competent DIY Mediation practitioner.

Once you've got to grips with the skills and process for DIY Mediation, you can test yourself with our online assessment. Get the questions right and you'll receive your DIY Mediation certificate. Details on how to access the assessment are in Appendix Six.

The case study

Throughout this book I'll refer to a simple case study which illustrates a typical workplace conflict. It is actually based on a real-life situation which in the end needed full mediation to help the participants resolve the conflict and move forward. I've adapted the actual situation (and obviously changed the details to assure anonymity) to show how DIY Mediation could have been used to nip the conflict in the bud. A transcript of key sections of the DIY Mediation undertaken by the HR manager, Mark, is contained in Appendix One. The scenario concerns Barb and Sue, two Sales Support Officers in a medium-sized company who have fallen out and are finding it impossible to work together. Their line manager, Chris, tried to address the situation by telling them to 'sort it out' but the situation had only worsened. Chris approached Mark, his HR contact, for help. As Mark had recently read DIY Mediation he was well equipped to support the situation!

I hope you find this book useful. In my daily work I frequently see the amazing benefits of using a mediation-style approach for those involved in conflict. If DIY Mediation helps you to benefit others in a similar way then I've done my job.

Section 2
Part 1
The Issue (what you should know)

Introduction

Before we get into the nuts and bolts of the skills and process needed for DIY Mediation, it's important to understand this concept we call 'conflict'. How will you start resolving conflict if you don't recognise it in the first place? This section takes a look at what conflict is and options for resolving it. My focus in the book is on practical application so I've split the section into two parts – what you should know, and what is useful to know. Of course I hope you read it all but if you want to get on with the skills and the process then I suggest you skip Part 2 of this section.

What is Conflict?

Negative vs Positive

One of the exercises we run at the beginning of our training workshops is to ask participants to brainstorm what words come to mind when they think of 'conflict'. Try this yourself now and I'm sure you'll find yourself coming up with similar words to the ones below which are the typical responses we get:

Disagreement	Dispute
Stress	Tension
Anger	Disengagement
Fight	Miscommunication
Frustration	Grievance

The common thread here is the negative connotations. That is a natural response, because our normal experience of conflict is of something that is not pleasant. Within HR, if we have to deal with conflict situations we are trying to minimise the negative impact for the people involved and the wider organisation.

Very occasionally when we run our workshop exercise we hear words such as 'opportunity' or 'resolution'. This takes a different view of conflict, seeing it in a positive way. If you think about it, we actually need conflict to be present for the organisation to prosper. Conflict involves people having different views and if everyone in a workplace had the same thinking failures would result. In order to develop and grow, organisations need their employees to challenge existing views, to think differently and generate discussion and debate. By allowing and encouraging this approach organisations will experience many benefits:

- Presenting different perspectives to ensure robust decision-making
- Fostering creativity, leading to innovation in thought and practice
- Open and productive communication
- Generating engagement through valuing diversity and expression of individual thoughts and opinions

If conflict can have such positive benefits why do we need to worry about it? Because what might start off as a positive can quickly turn to a negative. This is particularly the case when issues that begin as 'technical' disagreements become relationship issues. In other words it starts off with people having differing opinions about how to approach a particular issue but moves into the individuals having a problem with each other. At that point if it is not addressed and resolved the conflict can escalate and rapidly become damaging to those involved and the wider organisation.

KEY POINT

Conflict is inevitable in an organisation. It is how conflict is dealt with that will determine whether it is used as a positive to bring progress and growth to the company or whether it will cause pain and damaging impact to the business.

The Barb and Sue scenario I referred to in the Introduction illustrates the point I am making here. Sue is a long-serving employee and has seen the company grow over the years she has been there. She has set up systems and processes and for a long time was the only one covering the role. As the business grew additional resource was needed and Barb was brought in. Barb was recruited as she could bring different skills and experience to the role. In a positive environment this can have a beneficial impact on the business. Barb can introduce new ideas and approaches based on her experience elsewhere. Whilst this has been fine initially, Barb and Sue soon find they are disagreeing about how to do things – Barb is feeling frustrated that she isn't being listened to and Sue is feeling threatened by Barb. So a change that had been made to benefit the organisation and had initially created 'positive conflict' (challenge, innovation etc.) soon descends to 'negative conflict' as it becomes a relationship issue that is impacting the work of the whole sales team.

Is it a Conflict?

One difficulty is that conflict can have such a wide interpretation. Many of the situations that can be referred to as conflicts are not ones that we need worry about. Let's look at some examples:

- *Two pipeline engineers disagree on which is the best route for a new pipeline. Is this a conflict?*
  Whilst it is true they have conflicting opinions, most of the time good problem-solving skills will enable them to analyse the options put forward and come to a decision. So it is not a conflict which need concern us.

- *A talented young manager has taken up the offer of voluntary redundancy from his company and has two great job opportunities on the table, one with a top multinational, the other with an exciting new start-up. Is this a conflict?*
  He certainly has conflicting choices and he may feel he is in 'conflict' over which one to take, but with good decision-making skills he should be able to resolve the situation.
- *A project support manager in a large organisation has a stressful job with multiple projects running and big deadlines approaching and two project managers demanding he prioritise their projects. Is this a conflict?*
  Clearly there are conflicting objectives for him but with good prioritisation, positive communication with the managers and some sensible stress management he should be able to manage the situation.
- *A team member is picking up extra work as his colleague is taking time off work with a reoccurring sickness. He is complaining to other team members about the other person being lazy and selfish. Is this a conflict?*
  This has all the key ingredients of a situation with the potential to escalate into a relationship conflict so needs to be addressed.

Let's take a closer look at what these key ingredients are.

Conflict Ingredients

Conflict can arise in a wide variety of situations but there are certain core elements which you will find to be common to all workplace conflicts. Daniel Dana[1] identified what he sees as the critical ingredients necessary to make a conflict. Without one or other of these ingredients it is unlikely the situation will develop into a conflict that will need your help to be resolved.

1   *Conflict Resolution* – Daniel Dana, 2001

The four common ingredients are:

INTERDEPENDENCE	EMOTION
BLAME	BEHAVIOUR

Figure 1 Conflict Ingredients

I'll take a look at each of these and relate them back to the Barb and Sue scenario.

- Interdependence
  The people involved need something from the other and are vulnerable if they don't get it. This is often the case where those involved are working as part of a team or in a manager / team member relationship.

  The Barb and Sue scenario is a good example of this. Their roles are to support the UK Sales Team and to be effective they have to work together, sharing market information, updating each other on developments they are aware of which would impact the other. One of the common consequences of a breakdown in a work relationship is that communication deteriorates, meaning that information necessary to both is not passed on. This is certainly the case for Barb and Sue and as such they are both feeling vulnerable as they can't do their jobs properly.

- Emotion
  There will always be a level of emotion in the conflict. The situation is causing those involved to be emotionally upset in some way. Often this manifests itself as anger and frustration. It may not be expressed by an emotional outburst but in a more subtle passive / aggressive type response. Whilst anger and frustration are common there could be many other emotions involved, such as disappointment, paranoia, jealousy, shame etc.

7

Barb and Sue's frustration spills out into a shouting match in the office and this is the trigger for the manager to recognise that something needs to be done.

- Blame
  A strong element of an interpersonal conflict is that those involved each find fault with the other. The blame for the relationship problem is placed squarely on the other person and most often people will not see that they share any responsibility for the situation. As we see later when looking at how conflict escalates, once an individual has started blaming someone for an issue, a natural deterioration ensues. They will then look for further incidents or behaviours which will add to their 'case' against the other and justify the blame they put on them.

In Barb's first interaction with Mark, the HR Manager, she puts the blame on Sue, saying Sue needs to start including her more.

- Behaviour
  The final ingredient is behaviour – or more specifically the behaviour of those involved is causing a business problem. It could be that two individuals have fallen out but are managing to work together professionally such that their conflict does not affect what they do. If this is the case then it is not a conflict that we need to concern ourselves with. However, once their behaviour starts to have an impact which affects the business – fall in productivity, missing targets, damage to team morale etc. – then the conflict needs to be addressed.

In Barb and Sue's case the situation has been brewing for some months before it erupts in a shouting match in the office. By this point it is clear that whilst they have both been strong performers in the past, their relationship issues are affecting the team and so need addressing.

Recognising Conflict

You should by now have a good understanding of what we are talking about when we refer to conflict in the workplace but in order for you to respond to it you need to be able to recognise the signs.

Often the first time the HR manager becomes aware of a conflict issue is when the line manager gets in contact to say they have a problem with two members of the team. In many cases, if it has got to this stage then it is likely the conflict has already evolved significantly. We look more closely at the stages of conflict evolution in Part 2 of this section but a key rule of thumb is that the earlier an intervention is made in the evolution cycle, the easier it is to resolve the issue. As such it is important that you are aware of the indicators that could imply conflict is present in a team. If you have regular contact with that team you will be able to pick these up yourself, but it also makes sense to ensure the line managers you work with are also aware of these indicators. They are the 'front line' when it comes to identifying conflict and they need to be flagging potential issues as early as possible.

In terms of what to look out for I've split these down into two groupings which we can think of as Red Flags i.e. indications that there could be something that you and the line manager need to consider. I stress that there *could* be something. The Red Flags mean something is worth looking into further, *not* that there is definitely a conflict issue. The two groupings can be referred to as Activity Indicators and Behavioural Indicators.

Activity Indicators

These Red Flags relate to activities which can be measured and therefore monitored over time. Through monitoring, any significant deviation from the norm is an indication that an issue is potentially worthy of further investigation. I say again, it is not confirmation that conflict exists, simply a pointer to show something needs to be looked at further.

Table 1 Activity Red Flags

Activity Red Flags	Description
Attendance	Repeated periods of absence, particularly stress related; regularly arriving late; 'disappearing' from the office
Performance / Productivity	Fall in output of individual or team; unexplained drop-off in standards of performance, non-delivery etc.
Customer / Employee complaints	Increase in number of complaints received regarding an employee from customers and / or other employees
'Volunteers'	Lack of people offering to take on tasks when general request made; 'head down' mentality
Engagement Survey	Scores from engagement surveys show a downward trend on relevant engagement scores
Staff turnover / move requests	Increase in staff turnover rates and / or requests for departmental moves

Several of these indicators, attendance being the obvious one, are information which would be collated routinely in most organisations. If reported and analysed regularly it can give you as the responsible HR manager a useful starting point to discuss possible issues with the relevant line manager.

Behavioural Indicators

Behavioural Red Flags are indicators that are not measurable as they relate to changes in behaviour by individuals. As such they cannot be reported and tracked in the same way as Activity Red Flags and therefore rely on being picked up by those working closely with the person. The Behavioural Indicators fall basically into two types, 'evasive' behaviours and 'invasive' behaviours.

Evasive behaviours are associated with behaviour which is withdrawing and negative in approach. Examples are shown in the following table:

Table 2 Evasive Behavioural Red Flags

Evasive Behavioural Red Flags	Description
Avoiding personal interaction	Going out of their way to avoid people, limit face-to-face communication; overuse of email / written communication
Withholding information	Restricting sharing of information to purely what is required; 'need to know' approach, not volunteering additional help
Not returning messages	Lack of responsiveness; either no reply at all or long delay to reply; stalling 'I'll get back to you'
Non-contribution in meetings	Not participating in group conversations; refraining from giving an opinion and one-word replies to direct questions
Negative / withdrawn attitude	Negative approach to requests and trying anything new; not joining in group socialising
Less care on appearance	Showing less care about how they come across and even declining personal hygiene

Invasive behaviours can be thought of as the opposite to evasive behaviours. This behaviour can be seen as hostile or forceful. Some examples are:

Table 3 Invasive Behavioural Red Flags

Invasive Behavioural Red Flags	Description
Aggressive / argumentative	Arguing the point for the sake of it; giving unnecessarily sharp responses / demands
Shouting and verbal aggression	Rapid escalation of conversations into shouting; using verbal aggression; being impolite / rude
Undermining others	Being unsupportive and going further to put someone else down; spreading rumours and gossip
Getting others to take sides	Building coalitions against someone else; building a case and getting others to buy into and support their story
Game playing	Being manipulative; using authority inappropriately; sycophantic behaviour to authority figures

Naturally there could be a multitude of reasons for both of these types of behaviour. A traumatic change in an employee's life, bereavement of a close family member, for example, could cause these types of response. Equally there could be health-related issues, particularly mental health. So don't jump to any conclusions but use these Red Flags as a trigger for further enquiry.

How Conflict Evolves

You've used your Red Flags to spot potential conflict and you've seen something that needs further consideration. You need to avoid delay as conflict does not suddenly appear and then remain on the same level. It is likely to start in a very small way and evolve. The initial trigger is often something extremely minor, but unchecked and in fertile circumstances it can rapidly lead to deterioration. Let's look therefore at how conflict evolves.

We don't need to go into complex neuroscience to understand the simple lines our brain works along and how our feelings are impacted. The brain experiences a situation and will attempt to analyse it from a rational perspective based on past knowledge and experience. It will also have an emotional response, impacted partially by the rational analysis. Ultimately the combination of feelings and interpretation of assumptions will cause us to take action. The diagram below shows this flow:

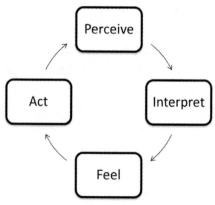

Figure 2 Perception to Action Cycle

To see how this works, let's return to Barb and Sue.

When Barb joined the company they initially worked well together. Sue helped Barb learn the processes, made sure she was invited to meetings and also helped her get involved with company social activities. The problems started when Sue noticed an email sent by Barb that she hadn't been copied in on but Sue felt she should have been.

This is the trigger point. Sue PERCEIVES something that has happened, albeit a very minor thing.

Her brain then naturally tries to process what has been perceived in an attempt to INTERPRET what is going on. We can only interpret based on information and experience to date. Where this is insufficient we start to add assumptions. Unfortunately these assumptions can sometimes be wide of the mark. Sue asks herself why she hasn't been copied in on the email. Normally she might pass off the situation as insignificant, a simple error. However, she's been having a tough time in her personal life over the previous couple of weeks and is feeling vulnerable. She thinks maybe Barb has done it intentionally.

The consequence of the brain interpreting a situation is to FEEL an emotion in response to the interpretation. Typically this is anger, frustration, confusion etc. Sue is a bit annoyed but doesn't say anything to Barb. At this point there is no action resulting from the Perceive, Interpret, Feel process. However, the next time Sue perceives something, her brain already has a 'negative scenario' on which to interpret the situation, based on the poor assumptions made on the previous occasion. This means it can add to the interpretation. This process can go on building based on what is seen – the 'case' is being built.

Finally, when Sue hears that Barb has passed some market information to one of Sue's sales managers, the interpretation crystallises into the belief that Barb is trying to get 'on her patch' and Sue's job is at risk. It has got to the point where she needs to ACT. She challenges Barb, resulting in a shouting match in the office. The cycle continues and both people are now in the cycle. They are spotting things the other person is doing / saying, interpreting it to fit their 'story', feeling the resulting emotion and acting accordingly.

Options for Dealing with Conflict

By now you have a good understanding of what conflict is, the signs to look out for and an awareness of how conflict can evolve. But what do you do when you spot a potential conflict? At this point it is good to remember that most conflicts are actually resolved by the people involved themselves without intervention from anyone else. As such it is important not to 'plough in'; making the right intervention at the right time is critical. We will look at a roadmap for appropriate intervention shortly but firstly let's consider the resolution options that are open to you.

Three Conflict Resolution Options

In any type of conflict there are three ways of resolving it:

• Power Contest
• Rights Contest
• Interests Reconciliation

A Power Contest refers to using physical or status power to resolve a conflict. In a conflict between two countries this would be the use of physical force to win a war. In the workplace power most often relates to authority. One way therefore to resolve a conflict at work is for someone in authority to use their status and power to decide the outcome.

How might this work in the Barb and Sue scenario? Chris, the line manager, could decide that the matter is trivial. So he tells them that unless they sort it out within a certain time neither will get a pay increase and they will both be performance managed. This may work but it could also have the effect of exacerbating the issue as it doesn't address the underlying problem.

In a Rights Contest the conflict is resolved by using some form of justice system. Both parties present a case and a neutral third party decides the outcome. This of course is the basis of the legal system. In the workplace this is represented by the formal HR policies, in particular the Grievance and Disciplinary processes.

Perhaps Barb raises a grievance against Sue for bullying behaviour. It would be investigated, normally by the direct line manager or another manager, who would decide to uphold it or not. If upheld, it may then be necessary to take disciplinary action against Sue. In other words it is a win-lose situation.

Often it is difficult in the workplace to be clear who is right and who is wrong, particularly with regard to relationship conflicts. That is where the third type of resolution can be helpful.

Interests Reconciliation is about finding a solution which as far as possible enables both of those involved to get what they need, i.e. a win-win. An excellent example of this is the Egypt – Israel peace treaty agreed at Camp David in 1978. Israel had occupied the Sinai Peninsula and was insisting on keeping some of it, whereas Egypt wanted it all returned. New borders were repeatedly proposed but none of these were acceptable. Only when the negotiators got beneath the positions of each side to understand why they wanted what they did was there a basis for resolution. For Israel, the key interest was security

– they didn't want the Egyptian army to be camped on their border. For Egypt, sovereignty was the main interest. The solution was that Egypt maintained sovereignty but put in large demilitarised areas on the border, thereby ensuring Israel gained the security it needed – an excellent win-win outcome.

Mediation is an interests reconciliation process. So if you use mediation in the workplace, whether through an external mediator or by putting DIY Mediation into practice, you will be aiming to reconcile interests.

How might this work in Barb and Sue's case? For Sue, it is important for her experience to be acknowledged and that she doesn't feel threatened by Barb. Barb's interest is that being new she wants to be accepted into the team and not excluded. Through the mediation process they find solutions that enable them both to meet these needs and thereby work effectively together.

Roadmap for Appropriate Intervention

As an HR professional or manager we have options as to how we address conflict. We have looked above at the three main options but how do you know what to do when? In Figure 3 I have suggested a flowchart which you can use as a roadmap for the appropriate level of intervention.

* Do Nothing
  The first decision is whether you actually need to do anything at all. Doing nothing is perfectly valid as a decision provided it is a positive decision that this is the appropriate approach at this point in time. It should not be used as an excuse for procrastination. You may decide that there is a good chance the people in conflict will be able to sort it out themselves and you resolve simply to keep an eye on it. It could also be that it is too trivial to worry about. Referring back to our conflict ingredients, for instance, if

the behaviour is not causing a business issue then we don't need to concern ourselves with it. We do need to monitor the situation though in case it escalates.

- Quiet Word

  If you feel that you do need to do something the next option is probably for someone (normally the line manager) to have a quiet word with one or both of those involved. Just making them conscious that others are aware there is a potential issue could be sufficient encouragement for them to resolve it themselves. Offering support if needed is helpful.

For example Chris might say separately to Barb and Sue, "Barb / Sue, I'm aware that you and Sue / Barb have been having some difficulties lately. I trust that you are able to resolve it between you but if you do need help let me know. Should it start to affect team performance I will need to intervene." Again, Chris needs to monitor the situation.

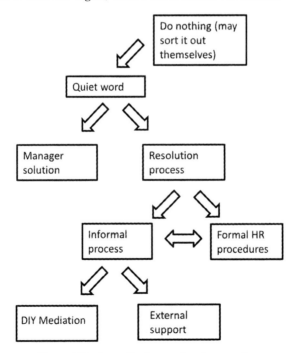

Figure 3 Roadmap for Appropriate Intervention

Assuming the Quiet Word has not been sufficient, you have two options open to you. You can use the power resolution and impose something or utilise a resolution process, either informal or formal.

- Manager Solution

  You may decide that a resolution process is inappropriate and that simply having a decision from someone with the necessary authority would be the best resolution. I'll give you an example from my personal experience of where this might be appropriate. In one of my corporate roles, part of my responsibility was Facilities Management, which included office moves. Moving people's location would often result in disagreements as to who would sit where. There would be little point in expending time and effort in trying to mediate between two people who both wanted the one window desk – not least as the situation could be repeated many times if there were multiple people involved. It was simpler to use authority to apply a decision, giving an explanation as to the basis of it.

- Resolution Process

  You discuss the situation with the line manager and agree you don't want to impose a solution (or this has been tried and didn't work). So you need to consider following a resolution process. Your choice is to take the formal route, using the standard HR processes, or the informal route, which gives you a number of different options. They are not exclusive. Often a formal process will incorporate an informal element as the first step in the process. Also, if you start down the informal route and discover something that means it needs to be formal you can switch. Likewise, you may pursue a formal route but the outcome does not resolve the relationship issue and you need to employ an informal approach to address this. So which route should you start with?

KEY POINT

Whilst it depends on the situation, a general rule of thumb is that if a clear right or wrong is needed then a formal process is better. If however the issue is not clear-cut (which is often the case with relationship issues) then informal would be preferable.

To offer further guidance Table 4 indicates the types of issue which would be better treated as either formal or informal, as well as giving some of the key features of the two approaches.

Table 4 Formal vs Informal Process

Formal	Informal
Types of issue	Types of issue
• Where absolute right / wrong is needed e.g. potential criminal activity	• Communication issues
	• Personality clashes
• Clear evidence of injustice e.g. discrimination / harassment	• Perceived discrimination / harassment
	• Differences in working style
• Clear disciplinary matter e.g. breaches of policy	• Inappropriate use of power / status
	• Rebuild relationships after formal process
• Major power / status differential between participants	
Features	Features
• Complaint on record	• Handled confidentially
• Structured investigation	• Informal discussions
• Laid-down timescales	• Timescale flexible
• Focus on past and establishing what happened	• Focus on underlying issues and how work in future

- Formal HR Procedures
  You've looked at the options and decided to follow the formal process.

Let's say that Chris comes to you saying Sue lost control and pushed Barb, causing bruising, and the scene was witnessed by one of the Sales Managers. A clear right / wrong needs to be established here, so a grievance from Barb is the appropriate route.

All workplaces should have a grievance process, so once the grievance has been formally raised the process will kick in. I don't propose to go through the steps here as each organisation will have its own procedure though for the UK they should all comply with the ACAS Code of Practice[2].

- Informal Process
  You think the issue is not clear-cut and agree with the manager it is worth trying an informal approach.

  Chris tells you Barb has lost patience with Sue whom she claims keeps making nasty comments and undermining her in front of the sales managers. Barb is feeling bullied. Chris has tried talking to Sue but it hasn't changed anything and he's not sure what to do. This sounds more like a relationship issue and you may want to make some further discreet enquiries, but it is likely an informal process could be the way to approach this.

Under the 'informal' banner you have a number of options. If you have read the rest of this book then you should feel sufficiently confident and competent to try DIY Mediation. If the situation is more serious (or you haven't had time yet to read the rest of the book!) then you may want to consider using a trained mediator. In large organisations you may have access to employees who have been trained as internal mediators; otherwise you can seek external support.

---

2   *Code of Practice on Disciplinary and Grievance Procedures*, ACAS, 2015

- External Support: Mediation
Using a professional mediator is obviously an option open to you and I would argue it is one that you should not disregard quickly (though being a professional mediator myself I am somewhat biased!). There would be a cost involved but as I show in the section on Cost of Conflict, the cost of not resolving the issue is likely to dwarf the cost of using a professional mediator. Best practice is that organisations develop a relationship with a mediator or mediation service that they know and trust. There are many people calling themselves mediators who lack training or experience. If you need to find a mediator, take recommendations from colleagues and speak to several. Whilst the framework for mediation is generally similar between mediators, we all have our own individual style and approach. Also their background may be helpful. Coming from a background in HR myself, I find this experience valuable in helping me understand what HR are looking for from me.

- External Support: Conflict Coaching
Whilst mediation is one of the most effective options for informal resolution, sometimes it is not possible to follow this route. As mediation relies on the voluntary participation of the people involved in the conflict, if one of them is not willing mediation is not possible. Also it may be that those involved want to try to resolve it themselves without having a third party involved when they meet. This can sometimes be the case with senior managers / board directors who feel they should be able to manage the situation without someone else, particularly a more junior member of staff, facilitating. For these situations another option to consider is conflict coaching. Conflict coaching normally requires several sessions and is intended to

empower the individual to engage in the conflict and develop skills and strategies to resolve it successfully. In the process a conflict coach works on a one-to-one basis, normally with one, but potentially both participants in the conflict. The coach will encourage reflection on the situation, seeing it from different perspectives and explore with the individual how they can approach the other person to address the issue. They will consider scenarios and test a range of options until the individual is comfortable with the intended approach and a plan is put in place. Conflict coaching can also be used for conflicts which don't even exist but where there is potential for conflict. For instance, if a manager has an impending performance review with a team member who is likely to be difficult, conflict coaching can help them work through possible scenarios and test out responses.

- DIY Mediation
  I've left this one to last as this is what the rest of the book is about, namely how you can learn a simple mediation-style approach and skills that will enable you to resolve low-level conflict yourself. As I said in the introduction, this is not about teaching you to be a mediator so that you can hand in your notice and take up mediating as a full-time occupation. It is about supplementing your skills and giving you a framework and tools to be able to nip conflict in the bud. How then does DIY Mediation differ from professional workplace mediation? I've outlined below what I consider the key differences to be.

Table 5 DIY Mediation vs Professional Mediation

	DIY Mediation	Professional Workplace Mediation
Time	The whole process is shorter than a workplace mediation. You should work on the basis of a maximum of 1 hour for each individual meeting and 2 hours maximum for the joint meeting, so no more than 4 hours total and often less.	Typically a whole day is set aside for the mediation itself. Prior to the day the mediator is likely to have been in contact with the referrer, normally HR, the participants and possibly others such as a line manager. As such time involved is probably 1.5 – 2 days.
Skills	Fundamental skills are needed but to a lower level as the situation is likely to be less complex / the conflict less evolved.	More advanced skills and techniques are needed. For instance, the ability to reframe negative language, handle strong emotions and explore deeply ingrained positions.
Structure	There is a clear structure and process flow in DIY Mediation and tools and forms to support. The structured approach makes it easier for a less experienced person to follow the process.	Whilst an overall framework is used the mediator needs to flex the approach. It is less linear than DIY Mediation, requiring the mediator to be comfortable with uncertainty and a more fluid approach to structure.

	DIY Mediation	Professional Workplace Mediation
Experience	Given that DIY Mediation is about adding to your existing toolbox, it is likely that as a DIY Mediator you will be less experienced than a professional mediator. You need to know your limits and call in a professional when needed.	Professional mediators, particularly external ones, will be mediating regularly and it is the kind of work where experience builds skills and effectiveness.
Conflict level	DIY Mediation is about nipping conflict in the bud. As such it is appropriate for low levels of conflict. Trying to address conflicts that have escalated to a more serious level could make the situation worse.	Professional mediators are used to dealing with complex cases. Avoid the mistake of leaving it too late to call on expert help because as time goes on positions become entrenched and even the best mediator may not be able to help the participants.
Neutrality	You will be dealing with employees within your own organisation. Even if they are not known to you, neutrality and impartiality are always going to be more difficult when you are all part of the same organisation. The same would apply to fully trained internal company mediators.	Professional external mediators have the advantage that they are independent not just from a mindset perspective but also in that they are not part of the organisation. This enables them to establish trust more easily, making participants more comfortable to open up.

The first part of this section has taken you through the key things you should understand about conflict to enable you to be effective in using DIY Mediation. You have a good awareness now of the signs of conflict and how it evolves. As to how you respond, I've given you some guidance on the options and an approach as to how to decide which option to pursue. If you'd like to delve a little more into the subject of conflict then carry on to Part 2 of this section. If you'd rather get straight into the skills needed to apply DIY Mediation, jump ahead to Section 3.

Section 2
Part 2
The Issue (what is useful to know)

In part 2 of this section I'll take a closer look at the types of issue that cause conflict, why it is important we deal with it and the natural conflict styles that we all have. My emphasis in this book is on practical application, so to be clear you do not have to know what I cover in this part to be able to use DIY Mediation. But a stronger understanding of conflict will certainly enhance your effectiveness so I'd recommend reading it – even if you come back to it after having read the next two sections!

Conflict Issues

What are the issues that cause people to fall out at work? An automatic response might be to think that money is a key factor for conflict – people not being paid what they think they are worth, not getting a bonus etc. This is not the case. Various surveys have been carried out over the years and more often than not those surveyed will cite personality clashes or different styles of working as the most common cause. The CIPD surveyed[3] over 2000 UK employees in a 2015 report and 'Differences in personality or styles of working' was picked out by 44% of the respondents as the issue behind the most serious incidents of conflict. Similarly a CEDR survey[4] in 2010 had 41% of people picking personality as the issue that would be most likely to cause a conflict. In the same survey only 16% said they thought they would get into a conflict about money.

There has been a lot of academic study into the sources of conflict but let's keep things practical and focus on developing

---

3   *Getting under the skin of workplace conflict: Tracing the experiences of employees* – CIPD April 2015

4   *Tough Times Tough Talk* – Centre for Effective Dispute Resolution (CEDR) – 2011

understanding of conflict to help you resolve it. One tool that could be useful in this respect is the work done by Christopher Moore[5] who identified five principal sources which he represented in the 'Circle of Conflict'. The relevance from our point of view is that these sources vary in how hard they are to resolve. Data disagreements for instance should be possible to resolve, perhaps through agreeing a common source or an agreed process. Values conflicts on the other hand have fundamental beliefs at the heart of them and so represent a greater challenge.

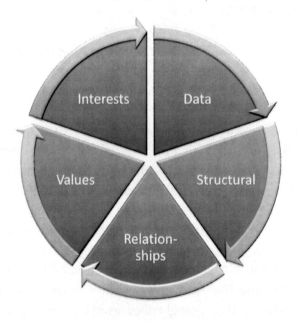

Figure 4 Moore's Circle of Conflict

---

5   *The Mediation Process: Practical Strategies for Resolving Conflict* – Christopher Moore, 1986

Table 6 Sources of Conflict and Causes

Source	Causes	Example
Data/Info	• Lack of information / misinformation • Different views on what is relevant • Different interpretations of data	Disagreement over figures in a report, interpretation of a policy
Relationship	• Strong emotions • Misperceptions or stereotypes • Poor or miscommunication • Repetitive negative behaviours	Two employees have stopped talking to each other
Structural	• Unequal control / distribution of resources • Unequal power and authority • Geographical, physical or environmental factors that obstruct co-operation • Time constraints	Two roles with overlapping responsibilities
Values	• Different criteria for evaluating ideas or behaviour • Different way of life, ideology, principles or religion	Employee who will work extra hours to drive for promotion versus employee who is more focused on work-life balance

Source	Causes	Example
Interests	• Competition over actual or perceived incompatible needs or wants • Can occur over substantive, procedural or psychological issues	Sales department selling as many units as possible versus production optimising plant running costs

KEY POINT

For the conflicts you encounter there will probably be a number of sources involved. However, what will be common to all of them is that relationship will be one of the sources. By addressing the relationship you will go a long way to resolving the conflict.

Needs and the Conflict Iceberg

We've looked at the kind of issues that can trigger a workplace conflict, but what is really going on for the individual? How is it that something which might appear trivial to an objective third party has caused that person to be so upset and has seriously damaged a relationship?

The apparent trigger for Sue does not seem to justify the response. She is outraged that Barb has given some information to one of HER sales managers.

KEY POINT

Invariably what we are presented with as the issue is only what is going on at the surface. These are the visible symptoms of the conflict but beneath the surface are a whole host of deeper, more ingrained factors which are causing the conflict.

We can think of this as an iceberg. With Barb and Sue we see them shouting at each other and making accusations such as not being included in communications. This is what we are seeing on the surface – the visible tip of the iceberg.

What we don't see is the rest of the iceberg which is a whole mixture of emotions, interests, needs, expectations, self-perceptions etc.

For Barb and Sue what we see on the surface is that they are upset about not being included in communications. But what is really at stake (which is beneath the surface) is what this means. They both want to do their job properly and be acknowledged as doing that and so they need the information. They have a social need not to feel excluded and a self-perception that they are valued by their work colleagues.

Figure 5 Conflict Iceberg

We can sum this up quite simply by saying that conflict occurs when people's needs are not being met.

> ## KEY POINT
> Our formal resolution procedures, grievance and disciplinary processes can fall down when it comes to addressing relationship issues. They focus on establishing right or wrong and are not geared to looking beneath the surface and establishing needs.

Through applying a DIY Mediation approach you are not trying to decide right or wrong, simply seeking to understand what is going on for each of the participants and helping them to find a way forward. This approach is much more relevant and effective in uncovering and addressing the hidden needs of those involved in the conflict.

Why Does it Matter?

We've seen that conflict is an inevitable part of any organisation and that it can be a positive force for change and innovation. Why then do we need to concern ourselves with conflict? Could we not take the benefits of 'good' conflict and just accept there will always be bad conflict and not worry about it? You could take this approach – in fact many businesses do, not necessarily because they choose that course but because they ignore conflict. This approach carries significant risk as the costs of conflict can be high and very damaging.

Taking risk is an inherent part of business. Business leaders are very aware of physical risks such as fire and flood and will buy insurance to protect against it. They are aware of market risk and will ensure their business plan addresses issues such as competition, pricing, demand etc. They also manage the risk of regulatory non-compliance by retaining accounting and legal expertise. But how many business leaders consider the risk to their business of workplace conflict?

> **KEY POINT**
> According to the CBI (2006) conflict costs UK businesses £33 billion per year.

Although the cost is significant, much of it does not feature as a line on the profit and loss account, instead being hidden in the cost of employees. As such it is a risk that often drops beneath the radar until such time as the business faces reputational damage resulting from workplace conflict, for example being taken to an Employment Tribunal or losing a key employee because of a relationship issue.

Leaders take steps to mitigate risks to their business. So what should they do to address the potential damage of workplace conflict? What is needed is an appropriate structure of policies, processes, skills and organisational culture. This overall strategic framework goes beyond what I can cover in this book, although the DIY Mediation approach is a key element. It is nonetheless worth having a solid understanding of the potential damage conflict can cause an organisation, which we term the 'cost of conflict'.

The cost of conflict can be split into tangible and intangible costs. Tangible, or direct, costs are those that you can actually measure. They can be broken down and turned into an amount of money that the business is losing as a result of conflict. Intangible, or indirect, costs are those that are far more difficult, though not impossible, to translate into a financial sum. They are however just as, if not more, important in terms of business impact.

Cost of Conflict – Direct Costs

A simple way to think about the cost of conflict is to consider what would be the typical cost of handling a standard grievance. I've often asked HR managers what it costs to manage a grievance in their organisation. Most have never considered it from a financial perspective and when pushed often say it doesn't cost anything. This could be justified from the point of view that no invoice lands on the desk (unless external paid for resources are used). However, significant internal costs have been incurred and let's see how these can be calculated.

To break down the different cost elements of a typical grievance, let's use our Barb and Sue scenario. Let's suppose that they go through a formal process as Barb raises a grievance to her line manager, Chris, against Sue for bullying behaviour. What are the cost elements involved?

Time

The most significant element of cost is the time of those involved both directly and indirectly in the conflict situation. This includes those tasked with resolving the dispute:

- HR representative (Mark) – receives the grievance and oversees the process, ensuring the Grievance Policy is adhered to
- Senior line manager (Jane, Chris's line manager) – manages the grievance investigation and meetings

There is also the time of those employees who are directly involved in the conflict, in this case Barb and Sue. Also to take into account is the time of colleagues who become involved through the grievance investigation and by Barb and Sue talking to them about the issue. In Table 7 I've broken down these costs using generic assumptions, some of which are based on survey data by bodies such as the CIPD.

Table 7 Cost of Conflict Calculation – Direct Costs

Cost of Conflict - Barb's grievance				
	Days	£ Rate / day	£ Cost	Notes
Time costs of initial grievance				
1 HR manager - Mark	7.6	270	2,052	a
1 Senior line manager - Jane	6.8	340	2,312	b
2 Barb and Sue	20	195	3,900	c
1 Line manager Chris	10	270	2,700	d
6 Colleagues of Barb and Sue	2	195	390	e
		Subtotal	11,354	
Potential additional costs				
Sickness absence cover	10	235	2,350	f
Legal advice	1	1,400	1,400	g
Replacement recruitment			2,000	h
Replacement training			1,500	i
		Subtotal	7,250	
Employment Tribunal costs				
External legal costs			4,000	j
Award payout			5,016	k
Additional staff time	20	270	5,400	l
		Subtotal	14,416	
		Total	**33,020**	

	Notes
a	£40K salary + benefits, o'heads; 228 working days; CIPD - 7.6 days / grievance / HR mgr
b	£50K salary + benefits, o'heads; 228 working days; CIPD - 6.8 days / grievance / HR mgr
c	£30K salary + benefits, overheads; 228 working days; assume 20 days
d	£40K salary + benefits, overheads; 228 working days; assume 10 days
e	£30K salary + benefits, overheads; 228 working days; assume 2 days each
f	Employee rate + 20% agency fee for 2 weeks
g	8 hours @ £175 / hour
h	CIPD 2015 Resource and Talent Planning Survey - median for non-manager employee
i	Assumed 5% of employee salary
j	The Law Donut's estimate for legal costs for 1 day ET hearing
k	MoJ, median payout for unfair dismissal in 2013-14
l	Average £40K salary of those involved; assume 20 days

Additional Costs

Often there are additional costs beyond people's time. In cases such as Barb and Sue's it is not uncommon for one or both of those involved to incur time off with stress and it may be necessary to bring in absence cover. If a situation has the potential to escalate to a tribunal claim then the organisation normally seeks legal advice, incurring further cost. Ultimately if somebody leaves the organisation as a result of the conflict then recruitment and training costs for their replacement are likely to ensue.

Tribunal Costs

The worst-case scenario in the UK is that the employee could take the company to an Employment Tribunal. The costs of dealing with a Tribunal case vary enormously depending how a company chooses to approach it, but for most the costs will be several thousands of pounds in fees alone before the additional time costs of all those involved are considered.

Our example shows that the total costs could be substantial, in excess of £30,000. Even if the only costs incurred are time related, dealing with a straightforward grievance case will easily amount to a five-figure sum. For very large companies costs can be significantly higher. The British Chambers of Commerce report[6] that one FTSE 100 company states each Tribunal claim costs £125,000 to defend.

But don't take my word for it, do the calculation yourself. Use your own average salary data and work out what the cost of conflict is in your organisation. You can work out what an average grievance costs and then multiply this by the average

6 *Employment Regulation: Up to the Job?* – British Chambers of Commerce, March 2010

number of grievances in a year to give you an annual cost for your organisation. Even if you don't have many formal grievances, you are undoubtedly called upon in HR to deal with employee conflicts, so you can calculate the time involved in these cases. This kind of data is the foundation of a business case that you will need to initiate any strategic approach to dealing with conflict, for instance introducing a company mediation scheme.

Cost of conflict in East Sussex County Council

Our Barb and Sue calculation in Table 7 is fictitious. However, one organisation that did calculate its Cost of Conflict was East Sussex County Council. ESCC employed around 17,000 employees over 500 locations providing services to a population of 700,000. As part of building a business case to establish a mediation team they undertook a detailed cost analysis of their grievance cases. The figure they determined (as verified by their internal audit team) was an average of £18,000 per grievance.

Cost of Conflict – Intangibles

If you have been involved in conflict yourself or in helping others resolve conflict you will know that its impact on people can be significant. For the participants, the issue can become their major focus and the 'ripple effect' will mean those around them are also affected. This impacts the organisation in two ways: decreased employee engagement, and business distraction.

Employee engagement has been a high priority in organisations in recent years and much time, effort and money is spent on trying to raise the engagement level. Conflict has a negative impact on employee engagement. If you are involved in or have conflict around you it drains morale and employees will disengage. Having excellent conflict management strategies within the organisation is therefore a beneficial way to invest in employee engagement.

Inevitably when conflict arises those involved are distracted from their performance objectives, impacting negatively on the business's ability to deliver on its objectives.

If a conflict escalates to the point where it enters the public domain there is a third intangible to consider, the impact on business reputation. Losing an Employment Tribunal for instance could result in reputational damage and deter potential future employees. In sectors where there is high demand for limited talent, companies cannot afford to miss out on the best recruits due to poor management of workplace conflict.

There is a final, very important point with regard to the cost of conflict. Leaving aside both the financial and the intangible negative impacts on the business, we must not forget the significant personal costs.

KEY POINT

Conflict can be a highly traumatic experience for everyone involved. We should regard it as our duty of care to ensure that we are minimising the impact of conflict on our employees. As such, it is critical that we understand what conflict is, recognise when to intervene and have the skills and processes to manage it competently.

Stages of Conflict Escalation

In part 1 of this section we looked at the Perception to Action cycle. But the 'cycle' description is not strictly accurate. It is more like a spiral. Each time the cycle repeats the situation deteriorates and moves down the spiral. Moving down the spiral the seriousness escalates and the options for resolution change. Figure 6 shows a conflict escalation model based on the work of Friedrich Glasl[7].

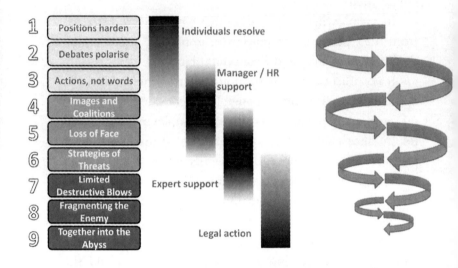

Figure 6 Glasl's Stages of Conflict Escalation

The idea put forward by Glasl is that conflict evolves in stages, each one more serious and harder to resolve than the previous. In the diagram I have shown what I see as the possible options for resolution. Early on the individuals should be able to sort it out themselves. If not they may need help from their Line Manager and / or their HR support. As things worsen, expert support may be needed, a professional mediator, for example. At the bottom of the table the conflict is such that the only viable option is to take legal action.

It may help to illustrate the various stages by looking at our Barb and Sue scenario and imagining how the conflict might have escalated had the situation not been addressed early on.

---

7   *Konfliktmanagement: Ein Handbuch für Führungskräfte, Beraterinnen und Berater;* Friedrich Glasl – Freies Geistesleben Gmbh, 2013 (in German)

Table 8 Conflict Stage Descriptions and Example

Stage	Stage Description	Scenario Example
Positions harden	Initial confrontation and positions form. Conviction exists that the conflict can be solved by discussion. There are no fixed camps.	Barb and Sue have shouting match in office.
Debates polarise	Thinking and feeling start to polarise. Perception of superiority and inferiority.	They try to talk and line manager Chris tries to help but fails, making it worse.
Actions not words	Begin to give up on speaking. Start to take actions – non-verbal behaviour dominates. Empathy is lost; danger of false interpretation of the other side.	Barb goes to HR to look at formal options. Communication in office is at a bare minimum.
Images and coalitions	Parties putting each other into negative roles; stereotyping. Seek support from people who have not been involved so far.	Barb and Sue try to get sales managers and other office staff on their side.
Loss of face	Direct attacks on moral integrity of other person, in public. Aiming to make the other lose face. A major escalation step.	Sue accuses Barb in front of others in the office of being a backstabbing cow. Barb posts on Facebook that Sue is bullying her.

	Stage	Stage Description	Scenario Example
6	Strategies of threats	Threats and counter-threats. The conflict accelerates through ultimatums.	Sue sees Chris and says has to get rid of Barb she will leave.
7	Limited destructive blows	Opponent is no longer seen as a human being. Consequently limited destructive blows are legitimate. Values are shifted; one's own 'small' loss is seen as acceptable.	Barb raises a grievan against Sue for bullyi behaviour. Sue raises counter-grievance.
8	Fragmenting the enemy	Destruction and fragmentation of the opponent's system is the main aim.	Barb accesses Sue's em to try to find eviden Sue talks to employm lawyer to see if she ha constructive dismissal ca
9	Together into the abyss	Total confrontation without any possibility of stepping back. The destruction of oneself is accepted as the price of the destruction of the opponent.	Sue walks out and raise claim against the compa Barb is dismissed breaking into Sue's em

KEY POINT

Conflicts that go beyond the earliest of the nine stages become highly damaging both for the people involved and the organisation in which they work. It is critical therefore that you spot the Red Flags early and intervene appropriately to nip conflict in the bud.

Different Styles of Conflict Response

We saw in Part 1 of this section how conflict evolves. First we perceive something; our brain interprets it in an adverse way which results in negative emotions and eventually an action will be taken. But what action is taken varies, depending on our natural conflict style.

We all have an instinctive response when faced with a potentially dangerous situation. The response is commonly referred to as the 'fight or flight' instinct. It is part of our human makeup. Think of a Stone Age caveman. When coming face-to-face with a prehistoric animal he had to instinctually weigh up, is this something I can fight and have a good chance of winning, thereby securing food for my family, or is there a fair chance it will eat me? In short, do I fight it or run away? It is similar when we face a potential conflict situation in the office, someone shouting at us for instance. Do we take them on and start a shouting match or do we absent ourselves and get out of the situation?

The natural response falls into the two broad categories of fight or flight, but much research has been carried out to look more closely at these categories and break them down into individual conflict styles. The work done by Kenneth Thomas and Ralph Kilmann in the 1970s is the most recognised and widely used of the conflict styles models evolving from this research. Thomas and Kilmann identified five principal conflict styles. The styles are determined by the level of emphasis an individual puts on the extent to which they strive to meet their own goals (assertiveness) compared to the extent to which they allow the other person to meet their goals (co-operativeness). Out of their work came the Thomas-Kilmann Conflict Mode Instrument[8], a simple

8   *Thomas-Kilmann Conflict Mode Instrument (TKI),* Kenneth W. Thomas and Ralph H. Kilmann, CPP

self-scoring assessment which enables you to identify your preferred conflict mode.

What Thomas and Kilmann propose is that we all have a preferred response to conflict. This is our natural conflict style (in the same way that we all have a natural preferred learning style).

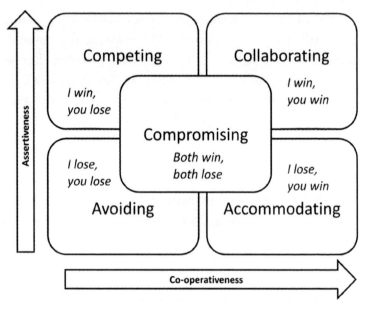

Figure 7 Thomas-Kilmann Conflict Styles

Understanding what your own preferred style is, will enable you to have greater insight into how you might typically respond in a conflict-potential situation. Through being aware of this and what the other styles are you may then choose to adopt a different style if the situation demands it. Equally, understanding that the other person in the potential conflict has their own style will help you respond more effectively to them. As a manager or HR manager an awareness of the preferred styles of the team you are working with is valuable information when dealing with conflicts between them. Let's look at these five styles and how behaviour can be adapted to work effectively with the different styles.

Five Conflict Styles

The styles can be represented graphically (see Figure 7) using the two axes of Assertiveness and Cooperativeness. I've described them below and given you an example based on the Barb and Sue scenario.

Let's say that Sue is having her annual appraisal a few weeks after the shouting match in the office and Chris, the manager, feeds back to her that her performance rating is going to be 'not satisfactory' mainly due to the ongoing conflict with Barb. We'll see how Sue might respond to this differently depending on which conflict style she operates from.

1. Competing ("It's my way or no way.")
Competitors prioritise their own goals and are less concerned about the wants and needs of others. Conflict for this group is about winning or losing and they will try to use their own power to defend their position and win the argument.

Competitor Sue's response to Chris might be: "I don't care what you think, you've got it wrong, and you are clearly incompetent. I'm going over your head to the director to get this changed."

2. Accommodating ("Let's do it your way, that's fine by me.")
Accommodators are heavily focused on the importance of the

relationship at the expense of their own goals. They will want to restore harmony quickly when conflict occurs and their need for being liked and accepted will override personal goals.

> *Accommodator Sue's response could be: "You're right, my performance hasn't been acceptable, I'll do what you want me to do."*

3. Avoiding ("I'm not getting involved.")

Avoiders cannot face conflict and will withdraw (physically and / or mentally) from situations where conflict arises. They are prepared to sacrifice their own goals as well as relationships to avoid the fear that conflict causes.

> *Avoider Sue will probably either say nothing or something like: "It's done, in the past; I don't want to talk about it."*

4. Compromising ("Let's split it down the middle.")

Compromisers will look for the middle ground. They accept that everyone should get less than what they want in order to find a solution that means everyone will get something.

> *Compromiser Sue's response could be to accept what the manager says but then go on a 'work to rule', just doing the bare minimum to satisfy job requirements.*

5. Collaborating ("How can we both get what we need?")

Collaborators work on the basis that conflicts can be resolved by meeting both parties' needs and maintaining relationships. They will take time to understand needs and generate possible solutions that will deliver what everyone wants.

Collaborator Sue's possible response would be: "I recognise that my performance could be better, but I'm feeling demotivated by the situation and your response to it. I think if you supported Barb and me to resolve the issue, I believe we could all benefit. That would increase the team performance and I'm sure the director would like that."

Adapting Conflict Styles

Perhaps you are thinking that Collaborator or Compromiser is where you personally want to be but remember, there is no right or wrong style. Different styles can be appropriate in different situations. Collaborating can give good win-win outcomes but it is very difficult to achieve and can take a long time. If a fire has broken out in the office you don't want everyone to sit down and discuss what response is needed to ensure everyone's needs are met; you need quick decisive decision-making. The table below looks at the five styles and considers the types of situation where each of them would be most appropriate.

KEY POINT

Whilst we have a natural preferred style, the nature of the situation that we find ourselves in will also affect the style we adopt. Someone who is adept at handling conflict has the ability to flex their response between the different styles depending on the situation.

Table 9 Conflict Styles – Appropriate Situations

Style	Appropriate Situations
Competing	• Quick, decisive action is vital e.g. emergencies • Unpopular courses of action need implementing e.g. cost cutting, enforcing unpopular rules, discipline • To protect against people who take advantage of non-competitive behaviour
Accommodating	• Build credit / goodwill for more important issues • Issue more important to other person • Maintaining good relationship is more important than goal • When you are wrong or losing
Avoiding	• When cooling down period required • Issues too trivial to justify effort • No chance of satisfying concerns • Potential damage of addressing outweigh benefits
Compromising	• For quick or temporary solution • Goals are only moderately important • Strong commitment to mutually exclusive goals
Collaborating	• Integrative solution needed, goals cannot be comprised • Where commitment from all involved is needed • Solution more important than speed of reaching it • Strong interpersonal relationships needed with understanding of underlying interests

So what style do you think is your own preferred mode? Taking the Thomas-Kilmann Mode Instrument assessment (TKI) will give you the answer but if you want a guide we have put a simplistic tool in Appendix Five which does not have the scientific rigour of the TKI but will at least give you an indication.

Understanding your own style is valuable but equally useful is to be aware of the natural styles of those with whom you work. This enables you to have some generic strategies on how to work effectively with them. The following table gives some general guidance on approaches that might work well with the different styles:

Table 10 Conflict Styles – Possible Approaches

Style	Possible Approach
Competing	• Give respect, talk in terms of their interests • Think about 'what's in it for me' from their perspective
Accommodating	• Recognise the importance of the relationship • Enquire in a non-confrontational way about their concerns etc.
Avoiding	• Alert them early to potential issues and check back regularly • Give them time to consider, don't rush them
Compromising	• Encourage them to take their time and not rush to a solution • Get them to find more information and delve deeper
Collaborating	• Check that they are aware of time and deadlines • Encourage decision-making when appropriate

A final point on conflict styles before we move on; sometimes the five styles are identified as animals. It is a good way to remember them and is particularly helpful if you are using the conflict styles with children. The animal names are as follows:

Competitor	→	SHARK
Accommodator	→	TEDDY BEAR
Avoider	→	TORTOISE
Compromiser	→	FOX
Collaborator	→	OWL

By now you should have a thorough grounding in conflict, what it is, why it matters and why people respond in the way they do. The next step is to take you through the skills needed when applying DIY Mediation and this is what I cover in the next section.

Section 3
The Skills

Introduction

This section guides you through the four essential skills that are required when putting DIY Mediation into practice. The four skills are Questioning, Active Listening, Assertive Communication and Impartiality. DIY Mediation works by applying these skills whilst following the AGREE model (which we will cover in Section 4), enabling you to support the participants in resolving their conflict.

KEY POINT

Applying the model without the skills or vice versa doesn't mean you won't succeed but having well-developed skills alongside good knowledge and application of the model will significantly enhance your chances of success.

Questioning

There are of course many different types of questions but here I focus on the key ones to use when running a DIY Mediation process, namely open, closed and hypothetical questions.

KEY POINT

Your questions must all be directly related towards the objective of the meeting, i.e. to help the participants find a way forward with the issues they are having with each other. You may feel drawn to enquire more about something out of personal curiosity, but resist the temptation.

Open Questions

Good use of open questions is one of the most valuable skills you can have in DIY Mediation. Open questions are ones which cannot be replied to with a simple 'yes' or 'no'. They typically begin with an interrogative, the most common of which are:

```
┌─────────────────────────────────────────┐
│   WHY       WHAT       HOW                │
│   WHO       WHERE      WHEN               │
└─────────────────────────────────────────┘
```

Figure 8 Open Question Interrogatives

Open questions are beneficial as they encourage the person to open up and speak about the issue. Early on in the process particularly you need to find out what has been happening, so using open questions will prompt the person to speak freely. Helpful questions in this respect might be:

"How have things been for you recently?" (Very general)

"What's been happening between you and X?" (More specific)

You can use open questions for a wide variety of purposes including:

- Uncovering feelings or further issues e.g. *"What impact did that have on you?"*
- Probing for further information e.g. *"What happened next?"*
- Encouraging a new train of thought e.g. *"Why might they have reacted in that way?"*
- Challenge a particular viewpoint e.g. *"What other explanation might there have been?"*

There are some open questions which are less open than others. The top three interrogatives in Figure 8, Why, What and How, are the most open as they allow a very general response. The bottom three, Who, Where and When, are less open in that the answer to them can be quite specific in terms of a person, place or timing. Therefore as a general rule use the bottom three when you want to add clarity and assist understanding of a situation e.g.:

"At the beginning things were fine but they started going downhill as soon as she got promoted, and she turned into a right bossy boots…"
"When was it she got promoted?"

Open questions, although a valuable technique, have their risks. For instance the participant can go off on a tangent, in which case you need to judge how helpful this digression is. If you feel the information is not adding value you must bring them back to the point, politely but firmly e.g.:

"Sorry, can I just bring you back to a point you were making a minute ago. You were talking about how you felt X was being aggressive towards you. It would be helpful if you could say more about that, please."

Here you are inviting the person to say more but using a statement rather than a question. This is another useful way of encouraging them to speak.

Take care when using questions beginning 'Why' as they can come across as intrusive or condemnatory. It is especially important to pay attention to how you put a 'Why' question. For example, if one of the participants tells you they decided to walk away when they were shouted at, you may want to ask:

"Why did you do that?"

Using the wrong emphasis or voice intonation might make this sound condemnatory to the other person i.e:

"Why on earth did you do that?"

When using a 'Why' question therefore it is often helpful to enclose it with 'softening' language e.g.:

"I see. Perhaps you can explain a bit more as to why you took that approach."

Closed Questions

Closed questions require a 'yes' or 'no' response. As such they are most valuable when clarity is important. This could be to pinpoint meaning when the person has not been explicit, or to check you have properly understood. For example:

"So are you saying that you have never discussed this with him?"
or
"Did he definitely use the words 'you silly woman'?"

KEY POINT
Be careful you don't use closed questions when you need more than a simple yes / no. If you were to ask "Was it an awkward conversation with him?" you could get the response "Yes". If however you ask "How did the conversation with him go?" the open question requires them to say more.

Hypothetical Questions

A hypothetical question is a 'what if' type question which is useful in a number of ways, particularly in challenging assumptions, promoting future focus and encouraging the participants to look at options later on in the process. It makes them think about alternative scenarios and possibilities.

In conflict situations participants make assumptions about the reasons for the other person's actions. Hypothetical questions can be used to encourage the participant to think of alternative explanations for what was said or done. Be careful when using a hypothetical question that it does not sound as though you don't believe what they are saying. Again it is down to intonation and body language to make sure you convey the right message. An example of good use of a hypothetical question is:

"You say she handed the report in late intentionally to make you look bad. What other reasons might there have been as to why the report was late?"

Future focus is a key principle of the DIY Mediation approach and hypothetical questions are a valuable tool to direct the participants thinking away from the past towards how the future could be. They may be struggling to believe that things will change but encouraging them to think how they would feel if things were to improve can often shift their thinking. For example:

"How would it feel if you could leave the meeting today having resolved your issue with X?"

In the Explore Solutions phase of the AGREE model you will be encouraging the participants to generate options. Hypothetical questions can be used to encourage consideration of other areas to explore. For instance:

"Okay, that's one option. What if that didn't work, what else could you do?"

Part of your role is to check how realistic the options proposed might be. This reality testing can be achieved through hypothetical questions. For instance, if the participants have decided the solution is to ask the manager for extra resources, a good 'reality test' is:

"What possible responses might you get if you put that to the manager?"

A key part of any agreement you reach with the participants is the mechanism for dealing with future issues. Thinking that they might fall out again is not something the participants like to consider but it is critical that you include this and hypothetical questions will help you to do so. For example:

> *"You have agreed a lot of things today which will help the situation between you going forward. What would happen though should you have an issue with the other person in the future? How would you like to handle that?"*

Questioning Pitfalls

A common mistake is to use multiple questions – where we ask a question but then go on to ask one or more further questions. Usually this is because we are trying to frame the right question in our mind and think we need to clarify or get further information. An example is:

> *"Can you explain to me why you said that and when you said it what reaction did you get and what did you think about the reaction?"*

Asking multiple questions confuses the person being asked and potentially irritates them as it can sound like an interrogation. The solution is to keep it simple and ask a single question. They may answer your other questions in what they say and if not then ask further questions.

Other question types to steer clear of are rhetorical questions and leading questions. Rhetorical questions are statements phrased as questions and will often give the impression of conveying an opinion. For instance, *"Can't you do anything right?"* It is central to your role not to express an opinion, so rhetorical questions should not be used.

Leading questions are those where the answer is implied in the question. Your role is to remain impartial and allow the participants to come up with the solutions, so leading questions are to be avoided. An example of a leading question is:

"So do you think meeting up more regularly might help improve the communication between you?"

Clearly in this example the questioner is suggesting the participants need to meet to improve communication. They however may have alternative solutions which work for them. So a better question would be:

"How might you improve communication between you?"

Planning Your Questions

As you become more practiced with DIY Mediation you will have more experience to know which question to ask at the appropriate time. When you are beginning though I suggest that you think through what questions you might ask, so preparation is important. It is impossible to plan the questions exactly, as you might for instance when conducting a job interview, as you need to have the flexibility to respond to what is said in the meetings. You can however develop some questions that you are likely to need. To assist with your question planning there is a tool in Appendix Four which offers some sample questions for each stage of the AGREE model. Going into your meetings having done some planning will mean you feel more confident and are likely to be more successful.

Active Listening

KEY POINT
The most essential skill when managing conflict situations using DIY Mediation is Active Listening.

When applied well Active Listening helps establish trust and rapport and greatly enhances communication. Why is it so critical? Listening is much more than just hearing. If the speaker feels they are being properly listened to they will be more comfortable about opening up and providing the information you need. Bear in mind that conflict situations often arise because of a breakdown in communication. Participants in the conflict have probably not felt listened to. As such, a key role for you is to give them the opportunity to be listened to properly and in so doing you will also be modelling behaviour that is positive for the participants to emulate.

To listen actively as opposed to simply hearing you need to take account of much more than just the words. Research undertaken by Professor Albert Mehrabian in the 1960s / 70s indicates that when someone is speaking about feelings and attitudes, their message is conveyed only partially by the words they use (as little as 7%). Greater emphasis is placed upon how it is said (38%) and the body language that accompanies it (55%).

KEY POINT
Active Listening is vital as it is the skill which focuses on all three major elements of communication
- body language
- voice and tone
- words and content.

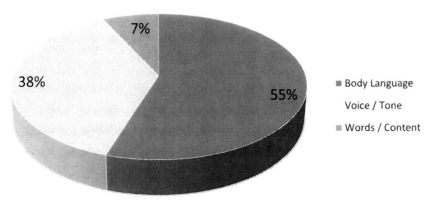

Figure 9 Mehrabian

The following is a useful definition:

Listening is an active process that entails hearing the words, being sensitive to vocal clues, to tone and pitch and inflection, observing movement, taking into account the context and communicating understanding.

Active Listening comprises a range of different listening techniques. It is important to learn and practise these key skills. A handy way to remember them is using the simple mnemonic 'REASSURE'.

R eflecting
E nquiring
A cknowledging
S ummarising
S ilence
U nspoken communication
R ephrasing
E ncouraging

Figure 10 Active Listening 'REASSURE'

Reflecting

Reflecting is playing back to the person what they have conveyed to you, often by using words they have used themselves. It could also include reflecting the emotions conveyed by what they have said. By acting as a mirror in this way you are checking your understanding of what has been said but also acknowledging the person's feelings. This may help the other person become clearer on how they feel about the situation.

It is important that when Reflecting you are responding to what you actually hear from the other person. Avoid trying to analyse, interpret or attach a meaning which might not be what they intended. For instance:

> *"Martin is always speaking to me as if I know nothing, like I'm a piece of dirt. It's been making me really annoyed."*
> *Wrong: "It sounds to me like you think Martin is on a bit of a power trip and likes to control you."*
> *Right: "You are saying you are feeling annoyed because you think Martin talks down to you."*

Enquiring

Enquiring is about using appropriate questioning techniques. We have already considered questioning as a skill in its own right but it is included under Active Listening as not only does it help you gather information but it is also a highly effective listening technique. Well-formulated questions help indicate to the other person that you are listening and want to know more.

Enquiring does not only have to be asking questions. Imperatives can be useful to show you are listening and want to know more e.g.:

"Tell me about how that came to happen."

Whilst this is not a question but a command it has the same impact as it invites further information to be provided.

Whatever Enquiring approach you use, *how* you ask is as important as *what* you are asking. Taking the example above, if said in the wrong tone it could easily come across as aggressive, damaging rapport and limiting your chances of getting the person to open up to you. If you think of Enquiring as being part of a general conversation rather than as an interview you are likely to adopt the right tone.

KEY POINT
Once you have Enquired make sure you listen to the answer and respond if appropriate. There is a real danger that you become distracted (see 'Barriers to Active Listening') so good concentration is needed.

Acknowledging

Acknowledging is conveying to the other person that you understand their position and feelings. To be clear, this is not the same as agreeing with them. Sometimes they might try to draw you in to agreeing but you need to resist. Retaining your impartiality is critical. It is irrelevant whether you agree or disagree with them but it is important they feel you are recognising what they say and how they feel about it. A good way to do this is through the use of 'I statements'. These are statements which begin with 'I' and Acknowledge what the person is conveying to you e.g.:

"Lesley is always ignoring me in meetings, only talking with the rest of the team and I just sit there getting depressed. She's not being fair to me, is she?"

"I can see you're clearly finding Lesley's behaviour upsetting," or "I understand you find it upsetting when Lesley treats you this way."

Summarising

Summarising is recapping the key points of what has been said to show understanding and to highlight the main issues. You might use some of the words spoken by the other person or your own words. The critical point is that you are not adding interpretation to what has been said, simply giving a much shortened account, capturing the main elements. Unless you have an excellent memory you will need to take notes to be able to Summarise effectively. When taking notes remember to pay attention to what the person is saying, make eye contact and don't bury your head in your notes.

As a listening technique, Summarising is valuable for a number of reasons:

- it focuses everyone on the key issues
- it demonstrates that you have been paying attention and have understood what was said
- it is a check for you to ensure you have understood correctly
- it organises thoughts which can sometimes be fragmented

After you have made the Summary a useful technique is to ask whether the participants agree you have summarised effectively. This gives them the opportunity to highlight any issues you may have missed. Summarising is a useful technique to use after a lengthy explanation and particularly at the end of an AGREE phase to make sure everyone is on the same page. Summarising can also be a very handy technique to use when you are not quite sure where to go next. It gives you time to gather your thoughts and making the Summary may highlight an area to focus on.

Silence

Silence feels awkward. Our natural reaction when there is a pause in a conversation is to 'jump in', to fill the gap and say something. Learning to overcome this natural urge will enable you to use silence as an Active Listening technique and, if used effectively, it can be one of the most powerful tools in your skillset.

From your perspective as the listener the key benefits of Silence are that it:

• puts the initiative on the speaker to carry on speaking
• shows the speaker that you are giving them respect by being patient (particularly important if they are upset as they may need time to recover themselves)
• gives you time to think about what your next question might be

From the speaker's point of view Silence can help them as it prompts reflection and encourages them to add to what they have said. Often after a silence valuable comments or information can come out. Whilst in theory Silence should be a very simple technique to employ, as you simply have to sit there and say nothing, it does not feel natural and so becomes one of the hardest to use. However the benefits are potentially significant, making Silence well worth the effort.

Unspoken Communication

Non-verbal communication is a vast subject that could easily fill a book on its own. To use DIY Mediation effectively it is important to understand a few key principles and techniques of unspoken communication and the impact of applying it well or badly.

As we saw in the Mehrabian '7% rule', when communicating feelings or attitudes over half the meaning of the message is conveyed through our body language. As such it is important for you to be able to pick up on the Unspoken communication being used by the speaker and also for you to make sure that your own body language is appropriate.

One of the simplest models for remembering key non-verbal communication techniques is SOLER, as developed by Gerald Egan. This describes 5 key elements which if applied will encourage the speaker that you are actively listening to them.

Table 11 SOLER Non-Verbal communication

S	Square	This is how you should position yourself. Facing the speaker squarely shows you are giving them your full attention. Make sure your head and shoulders face the speaker squarely. The rest of the body could be at a slight angle, especially if you feel sitting directly square could be intimidating.
O	Open	Your body posture should be open and upright to convey a feeling of ease. Crossed arms or stiffness will come across as defensive or tense. Your openness will help the speaker to be more open in return.
L	Lean	The third postural element is to lean forward slightly. Doing so will help convey that you are interested in what the person is saying, that you care and want to hear more. Think also where you position yourself. Give them sufficient space not to feel intimidated but not so far away that you feel distant.
E	Eye	Eye contact is critical to establishing good rapport and demonstrating you are paying attention. Comfortable eye contact includes knowing when to look away – staring can have the opposite effect to what you are intending. If you are making notes, ensure you balance this with maintaining regular eye contact.
R	Relax	Relaxing in front of the other person is essential to helping them relax. If you are fidgeting or looking uncomfortable they will feel your tension and find it more difficult to open up. Make sure you are feeling relaxed and that your body, especially face and limbs, are conveying that you are relaxed.

Managing your own Unspoken Communication is just as important as picking up on messages that the speaker is sending you through their own body language. To have a productive conversation you need the participants to feel relaxed and open. Given that the subject they are speaking about is likely to be difficult, they will naturally feel some anxiety. Your ability to build rapport through your own Active Listening skills will speed the process of helping them relax. Signs of anxiety to watch out for might include:

- avoiding eye contact
- fidgeting or repetitive body movements such as foot tapping and hand rubbing
- aggressive tone of voice, sharpness
- tense gesturing such as fist clenching

This kind of behaviour should lessen as the person relaxes. If not, it could be a sign that what they are saying is not aligned with how they are feeling. For instance, they are telling you they are over it and it doesn't bother them, but their body gestures suggest otherwise. A good way to deal with this is simply to reflect to them what you are seeing.

"I'm noticing that when you mentioned Bob's comment you were clenching your fists. How did his comments make you feel?"

KEY POINT
A warning – body language is only an indicator. There is no absolute definition which says when doing X they are feeling Y. By all means pick up on the signs and use them as additional pieces of information but don't try to psychoanalyse the speaker – apart from anything it will prevent you from listening!

Rephrasing

Rephrasing (also referred to as paraphrasing) is taking what the person has said and relaying it back to them but using your own words. The meaning is not changed so you should not be putting any interpretation on what has been said or imply any judgement in the words you choose. This is a really useful technique and one that can be used frequently when having conversations as part of DIY Mediation. It has a number of benefits as it:

- allows you to clarify and check your understanding of what has been said
- shows the speaker that you have been listening
- is a good way to remind you of the key points that have been made
- gives the speaker an opportunity to reflect on what they have said, and add to or adjust accordingly

A particularly valuable way to deliver a Rephrase is to use tentative words and tone as this gives the other person the confidence to revise what you have said.

The following are possible wordings to introduce a Rephrase:

"So if I've heard you correctly, what you are saying is…"
"Okay, so what I think I'm hearing from you is that…"
"Thanks, if I've got this right, you are saying that…"

Encouraging

The final E of the REASSURE mnemonic is the Active Listening technique of Encouraging. This refers to the wide range of verbal prompts and body language that indicate to the speaker that you are paying attention and that you are inviting them to continue.

In terms of verbal prompts these could be simple sounds such as *"uh huh"*, *"umm"*, *"ahh"* etc. or it could be short phrases such as *"I understand"* or *"Go on"*. Body language indicators would include nods, inquisitive raising of the eyebrows, perhaps accompanied by an encouraging smile. Often the verbal prompts and the body language indicators would be combined, saying *"uh huh"* while nodding, for example.

Combining Encouraging with Silence can be a particularly effective approach with people who are reluctant to speak. Once you have made your Encouraging prompt use Silence to acknowledge you are happy to wait for them to add to what they have said.

Barriers to Active Listening

Whilst high quality Active Listening is absolutely critical to making a success of your DIY Mediation conversations, don't make the mistake of underestimating how challenging it is to be a good active listener. Maintaining undivided attention is very difficult due to the barriers thrown up by our environment and the way our brain works.

Distractions

Firstly there are numerous potential distractions, both external and internal.

Try to minimise external distractions as much as possible by arranging a suitable environment in which to have the conversation. Use a private office where you are not going to be disturbed by interruptions and noise. Think as well about where you sit. For instance if you are opposite a window you risk being drawn to watch what is happening through the window. Consider also physical factors which might cause discomfort, such as heating levels, uncomfortable seating etc.

Internal distractions are also a risk. Make sure you are in the right frame of mind to have the conversation:

- give yourself plenty of time to have the meeting so you are not thinking about getting ready for the next meeting
- have the meeting at a time of day when you feel fresh, not tired
- plan the meeting so you go into it confidently and are not feeling anxious
- commit to leaving aside any personal issues to focus on the conversation

We all get distracted at some point so don't be hard on yourself when it does happen. You may find you have switched off and realise you may have missed something. If you think it important, be prepared to stop them and ask them to go back. Admitting you got bored is probably not the best way to gain their confidence but you could say something like:

"Sorry Bob, I'm not sure I fully understood what you were just saying there. Would you mind just going over it again as I don't want to miss anything important?"

Rehearsing

If you are new to utilising Active Listening or have not prepared sufficiently for your conversation, rehearsing represents a big risk for you. Instead of giving your full attention to what is being said, you are thinking about what is coming next – what question will I ask, how could I rephrase what they are saying, how might they respond if I said that? Have confidence that you will know what to say when the time is appropriate, especially if you have done your planning. Even if you do get stuck, you can use some of your Active Listening techniques to buy thinking time. Silence is the ideal option but also summarising of where you are will often provide a natural lead into what to say next.

Judging

We will cover Impartiality as a key skill later in this section and it is a difficult skill to master as both our natural instinct as well as our occupational training lead us to make judgements. Whilst you are actively listening, as much as possible switch off the instinct to form a view or make a judgement as to right or wrong, good or bad etc.

For instance, you may hear:

> *"When he demanded the report by the end of the day I told him he was a lazy shirker and he should write his own *** report."*

Your natural inclination will be to form a view about whether that was an appropriate response, or if you know the person referred to, whether you agree with that description. However, aside from needing to retain your impartiality, forming judgements is a barrier to listening to the person speaking and should be avoided.

Identifying

Again a natural response when hearing about someone's experiences is to try to make sense of it by relating it back to our own experience. The danger here is that you go beyond being empathic, i.e. showing understanding and acknowledging how the person is feeling, to being sympathetic. This in turn will make it difficult for you to listen impartially. If you feel sympathy you are engaging emotionally with the other person, thereby putting your neutrality at risk. So avoid linking back to your own experience and the emotional response that would result. Instead, empathise and acknowledge their experience and emotion without feeling it.

Problem Solving

It is natural when hearing about someone's problems to try to come up with solutions for them. As HR professionals and managers, employees look to us for advice and answers so it becomes automatic to analyse what the issues are and provide solutions. The danger is that when we do this we stop listening. We believe we know the answer and want to stop the speaker, save time and give them the solution. This is not the role we have in this type of conversation. We need to refrain from problem solving and instead listen, acknowledge and when appropriate, prompt them for options going forward.

Placating

A final barrier to effective Active Listening is our desire to placate. Our human instinct is to be supportive and make the person feel better about the situation. This we feel is good for them but it is also good for us as we want them to like us. To listen effectively we cannot get pulled in to the emotion. We can acknowledge it and recognise how they are feeling but avoid saying things which 'make it all better'.

These are just some of the many barriers that could prevent us from being a good active listener. It can be an incredibly complex skill to master as there is so much to think about including what you should and shouldn't do.

KEY POINT

The way to improve your ability in Active Listening is simply to practise. Fortunately it is a skill that you can use all the time. It doesn't have to be in a conflict situation. Try it out when you have conversations with friends and family. We all like to feel someone is listening to us, so if you improve your Active Listening skills it is more than likely to help improve your personal relationships generally!

Assertive Communication

The two skills we have looked at so far are centred on building rapport and developing understanding through appropriate questioning and Active Listening. With these you are pulling to you the information that is important. On the other hand Assertive Communication is about pushing out the information that you need to communicate to those who need to hear it. It is a technique that is focused on ensuring key messages are put across effectively and robustly. The technique can be used by you to manage the resolution process but also it is a valuable tool for those involved in the conflict. Very often their communication will have broken down. If you can help them to use Assertive Communication they will have a better chance of getting their point across without triggering the other person. By using it yourself you are also modelling how to apply Assertive Communication effectively. It is particularly valuable when you yourself are part of the conflict or potential conflict, the 'difficult conversation' type situation that we look at in Section 4.

Why do we need a tool to communicate assertively? In a conflict situation we need our thinking to be at its best. We want to get our point across confidently, express ourselves clearly and eloquently. Unfortunately the physiology of conflict is such that in a conflict type situation, emotions are aroused, the 'red mist' can descend and all the brilliant reasoned arguments that we might put across with a level head are superseded by emotional outbursts and blamatory language. As such, it is valuable to have a simple tool at your disposal which (with sufficient practice) can mitigate this natural response and enable clear, assertive communication.

The HEAR tool facilitates Assertive Communication. HEAR is an acronym for the four parts to the message we want to convey when we communicate assertively:

Table 12 Assertive Communication using HEAR

	Action	What you do	Why do it
H	Happening	State what has been HAPPENING in a neutral, non-offensive way	You need to be clear what the problem behaviour is that you are referring to. So you are likely to begin *'When you...'*. Keeping to factual language rather than emotional language will limit the potential for the other person to be provoked by what you say.
E	Effect	Describe the EFFECT that it has	It is important that the other person understands how their behaviour is impacting on you. So communicate in neutral terms how you feel or what you have to do as a result of what you have described in Happening.
A	Acknowledge	Give ACKNOWLEDGEMENT of the other person and their intention	Through acknowledging you are showing that you can see the situation from their perspective and are at least trying to understand why they are behaving as they are.
R	Request	State your REQUEST for what you would like to happen instead	The communication can only be effective if it expresses what you want to happen. Your request therefore should describe how you want the behaviour to be different from what has previously been experienced.

Let's look at the Barb and Sue scenario to see how Assertive Communication can be applied in practice.

You are following the AGREE model and are leading a Joint Meeting with Barb and Sue. Both have had their Individual Time and the conversation has moved on to addressing the underlying issues. However, they soon disagree and whilst they have tried to stay calm, they can't help themselves and start shouting at each other. You decide you need to intervene. An unskilled manager might blunder in shouting the following kind of response:

"You're both as bad as each other. I can't hear myself think above your screaming. Just get down off the ceiling, stop flinging insults at each other and start talking sense!"

This aggressive response could provoke them even more or mean they clam up and say nothing at all. A more effective approach would be to use the HEAR technique to intervene assertively.

Happening	*"Barb and Sue, when you shout at each other and throw accusations…"*
Effect	*"I find it difficult to follow the point you are making and I expect the other person finds it equally as difficult…"*
Acknowledge	*"I recognise that you are both frustrated and are trying to make your point…"*
Request	*"I would like you both to stop the insults and talking over each other and instead speak calmly and listen to the other person."*

By using the HEAR approach you are modelling the kind of interaction that will be more productive for Barb and Sue. You could also use this interruption to explain the principles of the HEAR tool and give them an opportunity to revisit what they were arguing about in a more positive way. (The break will also give them a chance to 'cool down' from their argument.) For example:

You – "Barb, you just accused Sue of being 'lazy and selfish for not getting you the information for the marketing report in time'. Could you try putting your point across again using the HEAR approach?"

Barb – "Sue, when you finally get round to giving me the information that you know full well I need urgently…"

You – "Barb, can I remind you that you are more likely to get your message heard if you use neutral language rather than blaming. Would you try that again?"

Barb – "Sue, when the information you provide me arrives late, I feel frustrated as delivering the marketing report is a key target for our team. I understand that you are under a great deal of pressure from the numerous requests you are getting and I'd like to hear your suggestion for what we can both do to avoid the team missing this target again."

Now Sue understands exactly what the problem is and the reason Barb is getting upset. By Barb acknowledging that Sue is under pressure, Sue is likely to be more open to agreeing to what Barb is asking when looking at solutions.

It may feel quite stilted when you start to use this approach, but after practice you will begin to express yourself more naturally. There is an added benefit. When you and the people you are working with start to apply the technique, rather than reacting in the heat of the moment, you will be forced to stop and think how you are going to say something. This pause in itself will help calm the situation and potentially prevent something inflammatory being said.

Impartiality

Finally let's look at what I consider to be the most difficult of the critical skills, maintaining impartiality.

What do we mean by impartiality? It means remaining neutral, that you do not favour one or other of the participants in any way, through how you treat them and how you view them and their stories. It is a major challenge as our psychology, our training and the organisational context all push us in the opposite direction, which is to hear, analyse and draw conclusions which favour one or the other.

Why do we need to be impartial? In Section 4 I will take you through the AGREE model and how to use it to help resolve a conflict. A key principle of applying the model is that you act as an impartial third party, a facilitator not a judge. The reason for this is that the process relies on the participants developing trust in you, understanding that you are there to support them and will not favour one over the other. If at any point they feel that you stray from impartiality, trust will be impaired and the process is severely compromised.

How then do you remain impartial? You need to start by accepting that in actual fact you can never be totally impartial. This may seem a strange thing to say when above I've said you need to remain impartial. The fact is that we all have inbuilt prejudices, both from innate instinct and learned behaviours. This is not a bad thing but a natural part of being human – we need this ability to categorise, make assumptions and presume to enable us to make decisions. In Stone Age times a cave dweller seeing an animal approaching had to make rapid assumptions about who was the stronger to decide whether it was the animal or himself who was more likely to end up as dinner for the other. In the workplace it is widely quoted that interviewers make up their mind on a candidate within the first couple of minutes of seeing them for the first time. What we are doing is taking on board a whole series of indicators that we pick up from each of our five senses and using them in micro seconds to form a view. Our brains will process all the indicators and assign categories to make sense of the information being provided. These categories will be based on intuition or experience. Referring back to our interview example, if the candidate walks in with heavy tattoos the interviewer will see this, process it and make an assumption based on their own prejudice and the context – it could be 'clients will be put off by a heavily tattooed receptionist' or 'he's creative and individual, just what the job needs'.

When applying DIY Mediation you will meet individually with each participant as the first part of the AGREE process. From your first contact with the employee therefore you will be making assumptions – categorising the messages you receive from your senses. In fact, even before you meet the person you will have started the process. The case has been referred to you, probably by the line manager, and when they told you about the situation and who is involved you will have started the process. The participants may already be known to you, so straightaway you have information based on your past experience which will start to influence you. If they are not known to you, as soon as you start to receive information you will naturally begin processing and assuming. What assumption might you make if the manager told you that the two people involved were called Josh and Phyllis? Your brain computes this information, categorising based on previous experience and you are likely to make assumptions about age and gender – Josh is probably a young male, Phyllis an older female. Not only have we now got some assumptions about who we might be dealing with but the assumptions will also link with emotions and our brain will naturally start forming pictures or scenarios. Perhaps Josh is a young graduate in his first manager role who has come into the team wanting to change a lot of things, which has upset Phyllis who has been there for many years. Or is Phyllis the battle-axe who has ruled with a rod of iron for 30 years and thinks that new recruit Josh is not treating her with the respect she deserves. We will naturally start to build these pictures and as we gain more information we will refine the assumptions and the scenarios that result. New information will come from a wide variety of inputs, including:

- personal appearance
- manner of speaking
- accent
- gender
- age
- seniority / job title
- what others have said about them
- previous personal experience of them
- attitude and behaviour shown

All of this data will be utilised by the brain to categorise, and characteristics will be assigned, both good and bad. This is an automatic process. We will assign a set of values to the person based on our categorisation and our natural response is to be more positive towards those people where the values are closest to our own.

KEY POINT

Whether we like it or not we all have these unconscious biases which will influence what we think and feel about others.

Whilst this may be a natural process it is also a risky process. The assumptions we make may be based on the best information available but they can be wrong. Many relationship conflicts start because someone makes a false assumption about why the other person has said or done something. When you speak to one participant you will hear their story and see the impact the situation has had on them. This will influence your assumptions and you are likely to come away thinking how awful the other person has been, only to find that when you hear from the other person there is a completely different perspective which leads to very different assumptions.

In our Barb and Sue scenario, one of Sue's major complaints about Barb is that she passed some information to Jeff, one of the sales people that Sue supported. Sue made the assumption that this was an intentional move to undermine her and encroach on her 'patch', threatening her job. When they communicate Barb explains that it was quite the contrary and she was only trying to help Sue out and had no designs on her job.

Our natural mental processes make impartiality a challenge, but as if this wasn't enough our emotional processes add a further hurdle. We all have a set of triggers which will prompt a positive or negative response in the individual. The Center for Conflict Dynamics at Eckerd College has identified what they refer to as 'Hot Buttons'. These are characteristics shown by individuals at work that could trigger a negative emotion.

We all have different hot buttons. Whilst one person may not be overly bothered by someone being over-analytical, this could be infuriating for someone else.

Table 13 Hot Buttons – Conflict Dynamics Profile – Center for Conflict Dynamics, Eckerd College

Hot Button	Description
Unreliable	Those who are unreliable, miss deadlines and cannot be counted on.
Overly-Analytical	Those who are perfectionists, over-analyse things and focus too much on minor issues.
Unappreciative	Those who fail to give credit to others or seldom praise good performance.
Aloof	Those who isolate themselves, do not seek input from others or are hard to approach.
Micro-Managing	Those who constantly monitor and check up on the work of others.
Self-Centred	Those who are self-centred or believe they are always correct.
Abrasive	Those who are arrogant, sarcastic and abrasive.
Untrustworthy	Those who exploit others, take undeserved credit or cannot be trusted.
Hostile	Those who lose their temper, become angry or yell at others.

KEY POINT

Think about what might trigger you. What are your personal hot buttons? Being aware of these will help you minimise the impact when you experience the hot button behaviour in the person you are taking through DIY Mediation.

If we accept therefore that we cannot avoid the natural process of making assumptions, forming opinions and being emotionally triggered, how do we remain impartial? The answer is to accept that our body and brain will be sending us these messages, be aware of them but *do nothing to respond to them*. Recognise what you see, hear and feel and put it to one side so you can keep an open mind and not be drawn into favouring one person over the other. This of course is easier said than done, so here are four tips to help you remain impartial:

Table 14 Four Impartiality Tips

Prepare	Be aware of any potential biases either about the situation itself or how you personally respond. When you are briefed about the issue you are asked to help resolve, maintain an open mind. As I have said above, you will naturally form assumptions so check yourself by asking what could be a different interpretation. Also prepare by being aware of your own personal triggers and hot buttons. We all have potential biases so be aware of them. By being self-aware you will mitigate the likely impact of the prejudice. Let's say for instance you are particularly sensitive to someone who is aloof and also you don't like tattoos, and the person who walks through the door is tattooed and talks down to you. By knowing that you have these sensitivities you can be aware of the natural negative response that you will immediately feel and put it to one side. If you are not aware it will inevitably impact on how you respond to the person and therefore jeopardise your impartiality.
Be aware of judgement potential and consciously avoid	In the same way that you should be aware of your own natural biases and emotional triggers, you should also be aware of analysing and forming judgements. During your meetings with the participants you may find yourself thinking *'sounds to me as though Bob's version is far more plausible than Bill's'*. Remind yourself that it doesn't matter which version is more plausible; you don't need to judge and it is damaging to the process if you do. So simply be aware that it will happen but put it to one side.

Be aware of own non-verbals	It is all very well for me to say be aware of your natural response but don't act on it; however the body may not be listening! As we have seen earlier when talking about Active Listening, much of our communication happens non-verbally. We need to be aware therefore of how our body is responding to what we see and hear. Even though you might be telling yourself not to listen to your judgement that Bob is more plausible than Bill, if your body language is more positive towards Bob you will betray your natural response and Bill may well notice it. It's important therefore that you retain impartiality not only in what you think and say but in what you convey from your body language.
Seek feedback	As we've seen, impartiality is a challenging skill to master. It is also difficult to know how effective you are in maintaining your impartiality. You may think you have done a great job but that is irrelevant if the participants don't think you have been impartial. It is a good idea therefore to seek feedback from the participants at the end of a DIY Mediation process as to how you have come across. Ask them to feed back specifically on whether there were any times they felt you were not impartial and what was it you did or said that made them feel that way.

In this section we have looked at the four critical skills that you need to employ when practicing DIY Mediation. Whilst they may be difficult skills to learn, you don't have to be a true master to make the process work, though the more accomplished you are in these skills the more effective you are likely to be. In the next section we will look at the AGREE model which gives you a framework within which to apply these skills, leaving you fully equipped to start using DIY Mediation.

Section 4
The Process

Introduction

This section introduces you to the process part of DIY Mediation, the AGREE model. I take you through the five phases of the model and the associated meeting structures. The framework is typically used when helping others resolve issues but can also be applied when you are, or could be, part of the conflict – what we often refer to as a 'difficult conversation'. We look therefore at how the model can be applied in this context as well as how to deal with typical types of challenging behaviour.

Background to the AGREE Model

So far we have looked at workplace conflict, understanding what it is, how to spot it etc. and the skills you will need to address and resolve conflicts. This next section gives you a process to follow, whilst applying the skills, to help move the participants towards a mutually satisfactory resolution.

The framework I developed is the AGREE model. Let's start with a definition:

> AGREE enables you to work as an impartial facilitator with individuals in disagreement, helping them find their own solutions and reach agreement.

Essentially AGREE is a simplified mediation process. When used together with the core mediation skills covered in the previous section you have a structured approach which serves as a simple practical tool to resolve low-level conflict situations. It provides you with an informal option which can sit alongside your formal HR processes to use when appropriate. As it is informal, you do not have the restrictions of the rigid formal procedures and the whole process can remain off the record. As such it can be an attractive alternative for the people involved.

The emphasis within DIY Mediation is on the individuals finding their own solutions with your support. You are acting as the impartial facilitator. This is a role which does not necessarily sit comfortably with us, as at work we are natural problem solvers. We like to help people by giving advice and the benefit of our experience. As HR, others look to us to make decisions and for guidance. When using DIY Mediation though we need to wear a different hat and impartiality is critical. How to remain impartial has been covered in Section 3 – this skill is fundamental to the success of this process so if you are not yet comfortable with it go back and reread the relevant section.

How did the AGREE model come about? In promoting my mediation practice I met many HR professionals and we talked about the kind of issues they faced and how they addressed them. One of the responses that I kept hearing was that the most difficult conflict situations invariably started in a small way but had not been 'nipped in the bud'. They had been allowed to escalate and descend the conflict spiral (see Figure 6, Section 2 Part 2). There was general concern around the competence and confidence of line managers to identify conflict within their teams and then to take action to address it. The typical reaction is one of avoidance. My own corporate experience, both as a line manager and working in HR, bore this out. As managers we received no training in conflict management and, as I suspect happens in most workplaces, there was no incentive to handle the difficult situations that managers are paid to handle. How often do we come across the situation where HR is approached to 'get rid' of a poor performer only to find that the manager has failed to performance manage the individual? All you see are appraisals with 'fully satisfactory' every year. Yet this is understandable.

How many organisations have reward-based objectives for managers which address managing staff performance? As a consequence, managers are unlikely to put time and effort into managing a difficult individual when they are not incentivised to do so and also put themselves at risk of retaliatory action.

Having been a line manager for over twenty years and now a mediator, I realised I had the skills and experience to create something to help managers and HR. It would lead them through a process, enabling them to manage conflict, effectively nipping disagreements in the bud to prevent them becoming major conflict issues. The AGREE model is the result of this. It is the kind of framework which as a manager and in my HR work I would have welcomed to guide me through situations which can be challenging, uncomfortable and damaging if handled incorrectly.

What is AGREE?

The model moves through five phases, from initiating the intervention through to resolution. The five stages take place during two sets of meetings together with preparation and follow up.

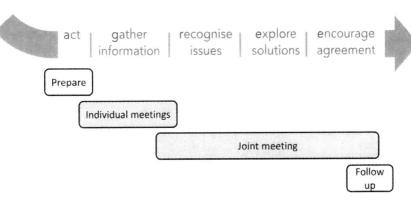

Figure 11 AGREE Model

The five process phases are:

Act	initiating the intervention and preparing yourself and the participants
Gather Information	hearing the stories
Recognize Issues	identifying the issues that need to be addressed
Explore Solutions	identifying options and solutions for each issue
Encourage Agreement	committing to action on agreed solutions and implementing

The first two phases of **AGREE** are covered primarily in Individual Meetings with each of the participants. For the Individual Meetings there are three key objectives:

- To allow the person to tell their story
- To help you understand what the issues are
- To enable you to decide the next step

```
Meeting Structure – Individual Meeting
– Open
      • Purpose and Process
      • Informal
      • Confidentiality
      • Impartiality
      • Future Focus
– They tell their story
– Summarise / check understanding
– Advise next steps and Close
```

Figure 12 Individual Meeting Structure

After Individual Meetings, if you decide it is appropriate, arrange a Joint Meeting where you and the participants meet together. The Joint Meeting mostly covers the latter three phases of AGREE and has three key objectives:

- To allow each person to share their story with the other, how they feel and what they want
- To agree and define issues to work on
- To find mutually agreed solutions

```
┌─────────────────────────────────────────────┐
│     Meeting Structure – Joint Meeting         │
│   – Open                                      │
│   – Individual Time (no interruption / 3 Fs)  │
│   – Discussion                                │
│         •  Trigger Point                      │
│         •  Issues                             │
│         •  Options                            │
│         •  Solutions                          │
│   – Write Agreement                           │
│   – Agree follow up and Close                 │
└─────────────────────────────────────────────┘
```

Figure 13 Joint Meeting Structure

Whilst A and G phases of AGREE are mostly addressed in the Individual Meetings and the latter phases in the Joint Meeting, there is inevitably overlap and it is quite possible that you will still be Gathering Information in the Joint Meeting or beginning to Recognise Issues in the Individual Meetings.

KEY POINT

AGREE is not a purely linear process. At times you may need to jump back to an earlier phase. For instance, you may need to Gather Information again when you have started Exploring Solutions if someone has forgotten to mention a key piece of information that is relevant to a solution they are suggesting.

In addition to the meetings the AGREE process includes Preparation and Follow Up. Preparation takes place in the Act phase prior to the Individual Meetings. Follow Up is included in the final phase, Encourage Agreement.

Let's move on to look in detail at the five phases of the AGREE model.

Phase 1 – Act

Intention: To initiate the intervention and prepare yourself and the participants for the process.

There are two key elements to the Act phase:

a) Preparation and
b) Opening the Individual Meetings.

Preparation

In terms of Preparation the first step is to make the decision that an intervention is needed and that you are going to initiate a process using DIY Mediation. How will you make this decision?

- You have become or been made aware that a problem exists by picking up on Red Flag Indicators (See Section 2 Part 1 – Tables 1, 2 and 3)
- You have considered your options with the help of the Roadmap for Appropriate Intervention (See Section 2 Part 1 – Figure 3)
- You have considered if DIY Mediation is appropriate by asking the five questions I proposed in the Introduction, repeated below:

- Have the individuals tried to resolve it themselves but are not able to do so?
- Is the issue causing the conflict non-binary i.e. there is not a simple yes / no or right / wrong?
- If not addressed could the issue escalate and cause further damage?
- There is no simple solution that could be implemented which would fully resolve the issue?
- Do you feel sufficiently competent and confident to start the process?

Figure 14 5 Questions – Is DIY Mediation appropriate?

As a result you decide you need to address the situation using DIY Mediation and are going to initiate the **AGREE** process.

The next step is to arrange the Individual Meetings with the individuals concerned. Set aside an hour for each of these meetings and think about the timing. It could be a difficult, emotional or unsettling meeting for the employee – and for you for that matter. So avoid the typical 'bad' times for this kind of meeting, such as:

- Right at the end of the day
- Just before the weekend
- Just before they go on holiday

Make sure you won't be disturbed. Plan to turn your phone off and make sure any colleagues who need to know are aware you are in a confidential meeting and should not be interrupted. Also find a suitable location for the meeting. A private room or office is important to ensure no conversation will be overheard and confidentiality can be maintained.

The final point on Preparation is to make sure you have prepared *yourself* for the meeting. Think through how you are going to open the meeting, some possible questions and how you will structure it (structure is covered later in this section). Just as important as *what* you are going to say is *how* you are going to be. You will need to be calm, positive and non-judgemental.

KEY POINT
Remaining calm is essential. You could hear things which annoy, upset or frustrate you. It's even possible that the situation gets turned against you... 'If only you lot in HR would do something about him... etc.' Think through how you will remain calm and avoid being pulled into the emotion of the situation.

Consider too how you will maintain a positive outlook. It is part of your role to encourage belief in a positive outcome to the process and to make sure the participants focus on the future and not just on what has gone on in the past. As such, you will need to maintain your own positivity – have confidence that you have the skills and tools to help resolve the situation.

Finally, remind yourself about impartiality. As you hear the person's story it is natural that you will start to make assumptions and judgements – we all do this, so don't be critical of yourself for doing so. However, try as much as possible to limit those judgements, reminding yourself you are hearing one person's perspective. No matter how convincing they sound there is always another side to the story. Remember that your purpose in this process is not to decide who is right and wrong but to help the participants find a way out of their disagreement and agree on how they will work together going forward.

For Preparation therefore you have set up the meetings at a convenient time and place, allowing sufficient time. Prior to the meeting you have prepared yourself so you can maintain your calm and your positive, non-judgemental approach.

Opening the Individual Meeting

It is helpful at the beginning of this one-to-one meeting to give a brief opening to explain the meeting to the other person. Bear in mind that they probably don't know much about the meeting, and may well be quite concerned. After all, being asked by HR to attend a meeting to discuss a difficult workplace relationship is unlikely to be a usual or comfortable experience. It is vital therefore that from the start of the meeting you build rapport and help calm them. Your degree of success in helping them resolve the issue will depend largely on the level of trust you establish and how comfortable they are to open up. So establishing trust early on is critical.

After initial greetings and rapport building, give a brief opening which should cover the following:

- Purpose and Process
- Informal and Confidential
- Impartiality
- Future Focus

Let's look at each of these.

Purpose and Process

Be clear what the meeting is about and how you see the process going forward. This type of meeting will not be familiar to the other person, so make sure they understand why they are there and what you are intending to do. Mention how you have become aware of the situation and what process you are proposing. In the Barb and Sue scenario, Mark, the HR manager, opens his Individual Meeting with Barb as follows:

"Barb, thanks for having a chat with me this morning. What it's about is that I've been speaking with Chris and he has noticed recently that you and Sue have not been getting along that well. We are concerned about the impact that might be having on both of you. So Chris has asked for my help. What we'd like to do is support you both to work through any issues you are having as none of us want things to escalate and potentially impact badly on the team's work. So I'm going to meet with you and Sue separately and probably then the three of us can get together to find some ways forward. How does that sound? "

Informal and Confidential

The employee could be concerned that this is the beginning of a formal HR process. You need to be clear that the process you are proposing is informal. As such it remains off the record; no note will appear in their personnel file and they can choose to participate or not. No-one is compelling them to take part in the process but you need to indicate that the organisation wants the situation resolved and this process is intended to do that. You can also make it clear that both the employee and the organisation still have access to the formal HR procedures at any point should the informal approach not succeed.

Stress that the conversations during the process remain confidential. No information is shared outside of the meetings unless agreed in the meetings. You commit yourself to this but also expect the employees involved to respect this confidentiality. It is in their own interests to maintain the confidentiality which is one of the benefits of an informal process. This means the individuals involved can resolve the problem without pulling in other team members etc. for interview as would be necessary in a formal grievance or disciplinary process.

> **KEY POINT**
> The commitment to confidentiality extends only so far as corporate policy will allow. If for instance you were to hear in the course of the conversations that a major breach of policy has been committed, an admission of fraud, for example, you would be obliged to report it. As such, be sure to say you retain the right to terminate the informal approach if necessary.

Impartiality

It is essential you make it clear you are acting as an independent, impartial facilitator. Participants will be expecting the 'normal' HR approach of acting as arbiter on right and wrong, giving advice or instruction and offering solutions. You need to emphasise you are wearing a different hat and consequently you will not be favouring one or other of the people involved, and you will not be solving the problem for them. You are expecting them to work together to find a way forward and you will support and facilitate this process.

Future Focus

Finally, clarify for them that the core intention of the process is to focus on how things will work better in the future. In order to do this, there will have to be a consideration of what has happened in the past.

> **KEY POINT**
> Past issues are discussed to understand what went on, clarify misconceptions and to identify what needs to be addressed to make things better going forward. It is not about deciding the rights or wrongs of whatever happened.

Summary

On opening Individual Meetings you are aiming to settle the person down and talk to them about how the process will work, making sure they understand that it is informal, confidential and future focused and that you are there as an impartial facilitator. After your opening, check with them that they are clear on what you have said and see if they have any questions. Remember, this is a different type of meeting to what they may have been expecting so it is vital that they are comfortable with the proposed approach.

Phase 2 – Gather Information

Intention: To allow each participant to tell their story, vent feelings and say what they want for the future.

Most of this phase takes place during the two Individual Meetings with each of the participants, although gathering information could happen at any stage of the process.

In the Act phase you opened the Individual Meeting and answered any questions the participants might have. You now need to allow them the opportunity to tell their story and encourage them to do so with an invitation, such as:

> *'I'd like to hear about the situation as you see it…' or 'Tell me what's been going on for you…'*

You are looking to hear what I think of as the 'Three Fs'

FACTS   FEELINGS   FUTURE

- *Facts* – what has happened as they see it? This will be *their* version of the situation. When you see the other person you may well get a very different version. This does not matter as you are not attempting to decide whose version is right or wrong, and who you believe or disbelieve. The purpose of hearing what has happened is to help you decide on the process going forward (is a Joint Meeting appropriate for instance) and for them to feel listened to.

- *Feelings* – how do they feel about the situation? They may not express this directly so you may have to probe with questions such as:

'*How did you feel when they did that...?*'

If you sense they might be uncomfortable talking about feelings you could approach this another way and talk instead about the effect it has had on them e.g.:

'*How did it impact on you when she said that...?*'

If they are struggling to express themselves, a useful tool is a reflective statement. In other words, say what you are seeing to give them a prompt e.g.:

'*What's coming across to me is that you appear quite angry that she responded to you in that way...*'

Why is this important? By saying how they feel about the situation they have to stand back from it and consider how they have been affected. Acknowledging this is a positive step towards finding a way out of the situation.

- *Future* – what do they see as the way forward? The purpose of the process is to find how the people involved can work together in the future. As such, even at this early stage you need to shift their thinking towards the future and how it could be. This will develop positivity and start the brain thinking about solutions. It is unlikely they will start talking about the future unprompted, so you need to encourage them. Helpful questions could be:

'What might work for you?' or 'If you could imagine a way forward, what might it be?'

KEY POINT

In my experience participants are often very willing to give you plenty of 'Facts', but they are less inclined to talk about 'Feelings' and will almost certainly need to be prompted to talk about 'Future'. However it is the last two that are the most important for this process. Therefore a crucial part of your role is to ensure that 'Feelings' and 'Future' get heard as well as 'Facts'.

Be wary of getting too involved in the detail of the story. It is quite possible they want to 'prove their case'. Don't be surprised if they turn up to the Individual Meeting with a wad of documents as evidence. It is important they understand you would like to hear the story in their own words. If it helps to understand the situation you could look briefly at a document but you are not there to pass judgement on anything they show or tell you.

The key skill you apply at this phase is Active Listening so remind yourself of the key techniques before you start the Individual Meetings. If you are uncertain have the REASSURE framework in front of you as a reminder during the meeting. Effective application of Active Listening is critical to establishing rapport and trust with the other person. Only through building trust will they feel comfortable to open up to you. You can then probe beneath the surface to explore what might be going on but is hidden, thereby establishing the needs and interests that are not being met.

Establishing Needs and Interests

As we established in Section 2, conflict arises when an individual's needs are not being met. To facilitate resolution therefore, it is very helpful to understand what those needs are. Solutions that meet the needs of all those involved in the conflict are the ideal outcome – a true win-win. The approach we adopt in DIY Mediation facilitates a collaborative process to achieve this.

What do I mean by this? The following well-known example is a great illustration. Two sisters are fighting over an orange. There is only one orange and they both say they want it. They say things such as *'I want it, you can't have it, it's my turn, I need it more than you, you can have something else etc.'* Mother comes in and asks why they are fighting. They tell her and each ask mother to give them the orange. Mother could listen to them both and decide who to give it to. Instead she asks them both to explain why they want the orange. It turns out that one sister wants to squeeze the orange to make orange juice whilst the other wants to make a cake so needs the orange peel. Mother peels the orange, gives the peel to one and the fruit to the other so both their needs are met.

This story illustrates the value of digging beneath 'what' people say to find out 'why' they are saying it. We think of this as their 'position' (the what) compared to their 'needs and interests' (the why). Very often, in the Gather Information phase what we will be hearing is the position of the person. Figure 5 in Section 2 Part 2 illustrates this diagrammatically. If we think of an iceberg, what they tell us (the position) is what we see, i.e. the tip of the iceberg. What is hidden from us is a mass of underlying interests made up of many things such as concerns, fears, desires, motivations etc. By appropriate questioning and probing we can identify the underlying needs and interests.

> *In the Barb and Sue scenario, when Mark meets with Sue in the Individual Meeting, Sue expresses a position when she talks about Barb creeping onto her patch, taking over her job and wanting her moved. Through Mark's questioning it becomes clear why Sue is taking this position. She is feeling undermined, threatened and also aggrieved that her friend did not get the job. So her needs are to feel secure in her role and for clarity in understanding why Barb got the job she thought should go to her friend.*

Understanding the underlying needs and interests is valuable in the later phases of the model. When it comes to proposed solutions, checking whether those solutions satisfy the needs identified is a good test of how effective they will be.

Closing the Individual Meeting

Once they have told you their story and you have probed further with appropriate questions you should have a good view on the three Fs:

- what they see has happened – Facts
- what they feel about it – Feelings
- and what they'd like to happen – Future

You will also have started to get an idea of both:

- what the *issues* are that you will need to address when you meet in the Joint Meeting

- what the *needs and interests* are of the individual that will need to be addressed in any proposed solutions

KEY POINT

Before you close the Individual Meeting you must summarise back to participants what they have said. This helps clarify the key points in your mind but also allows them to reflect if there is anything they have missed.

Check your understanding of what you have heard – phrases such as *'So what I'm hearing is…'* are helpful in this context. Finally make sure you ask them if there is anything else they want to tell you at this stage.

You should close the meeting by advising them of what will happen next, i.e. after you have seen them both you will be looking at how to take this forward. The most likely route is that you will arrange a Joint Meeting where the three of you will meet to resolve the issues. You should briefly outline how the Joint Meeting is structured, suggesting they have a think about the Individual Time and what they would like to say. Answer any concerns they might have about the meeting.

What if they don't want to do a Joint Meeting?
- Explore with them what their concerns are and try to address them
- Tell them about the process and clarify anything they are unsure about
- Talk through the options open to them if they don't go down this route
- Emphasise that the organisation wants the issue resolved and that this approach will allow a solution which they agree with the other person
- Encourage them to consider the 'risks' of not doing it

Figure 15 What if they don't want to do a Joint Meeting?

Next Step

After meeting both individuals your task is to decide on what to do next. You have a range of options, the key ones being:

- Continue to a Joint Meeting
- Switch to a different process
- Stop the process

The most likely outcome is that you proceed to a Joint Meeting. Provided you have not heard anything in the Individual Meetings that causes you to think a Joint Meeting would not be productive, or even exacerbate the issue, then this is the route to follow. Examples of issues that could suggest an alternative to a Joint Meeting is needed:

- You have heard something which indicates that a formal process is required, e.g. a serious breach of policy
- You believe one or both the participants would not cope with facing each other and might put their wellbeing at risk
- You are not sufficiently confident in your own ability to manage a Joint Meeting and need more specialist support
- You decide the issue is not as serious as was indicated and by not doing anything it is likely to go away whereas discussing it could make it worse (NB. This may be a tempting but risky approach. Be absolutely sure therefore that such an approach is taken for the right reasons and is not simply avoiding the issue.)

In terms of switching to a different process, you have the formal HR processes available to you. You might decide this is the way to go if a clear right / wrong is needed – for instance you have heard a serious and credible argument that bullying has occurred, or a substantiated allegation of fraudulent activity.

Another option is to seek more specialist assistance. You may decide that the situation is particularly delicate or critical and needs someone with expert skills. You could in this instance refer it to an external mediator.

Assuming you decide to proceed to a Joint Meeting, set the meeting up taking account of the same factors considered when arranging the Individual Meetings e.g. timing, location etc. You should allow up to two hours for the meeting.

Summary

For the Gather Information phase you have heard from each individual what their story is, how they feel about it and what they would like to happen. You have probed to understand better what the issues are and have gained an idea of their underlying needs and interests. You have closed the meeting, advising of what will happen next and then made a decision on the next stage of the process, including, if appropriate, arranging the Joint Meeting.

Phase 3 – Recognise Issues

Intention: To identify the issues that need to be addressed to resolve the conflict

This phase will happen primarily during the early stages of the Joint Meeting, though it is likely you already have an idea of what the issues could be based on the Individual Meetings.

Joint Meeting – Preparation

Before the Joint Meeting ensure you do any necessary preparation. As with the Individual Meetings you need to prepare yourself in terms of the attitude you take into the meeting, reminding yourself about impartiality, positive focus etc.

> **KEY POINT**
>
> Your role in this meeting is the Process manager. You are not there to decide, advise or problem solve – you need to facilitate the process that will enable the individuals involved to come to their own agreements.

You should think through the meeting structure (see Figure 13) and plan accordingly:

- What are you going to say at the opening of the meeting?
- Have you considered possible questions? You may want to look at the Sample Questions (Appendix Four) if you want some pointers as to potential questions.
- You are aiming to have an agreement at the end of the meeting, so how will this be done? Do you want to prepare a template before the meeting? You may wish to base it on the Agreement Example (Appendix Two).

Joint Meeting – Opening

Begin the meeting by reminding the participants about the purpose of the meeting, your role and your expectations of them. For example:

> *'Barb and Sue, thanks for meeting me here today. I've had a chance to speak with you individually about the issues that have been affecting you in recent weeks. Today I'd like to work with you, supporting you to find your own solutions to these issues that enable you to move forward and work effectively together.'*

Remind them also about confidentiality. They should feel comfortable to speak openly as they will only be able to reach robust agreement if they are open and honest with each other. You can give them your commitment that you will keep the conversations confidential unless you are made aware of anything that under company policy you would be obliged to report. Likewise ask them to commit to keeping all they hear in the meetings confidential.

Should confidentiality be of particular concern to one or both participants, a good solution is to include the confidentiality commitment as part of the final agreement. They are then both clear on what they can and can't say outside of the meeting.

Give them a brief indication of the meeting structure and check if they have any questions before you proceed.

Joint Meeting – Individual Time

In the first stage of the Joint Meeting give each of the participants Individual Time. This is their opportunity to speak, giving their own perspective on the situation. Encourage them to talk about the three Fs (Facts, Feelings and Future), i.e. what has happened, how it has impacted them and what they would like to happen going forward. Give them a maximum of 10 minutes each for this.

A key part of Individual Time is that it is *uninterrupted*. If the other person interrupts you need to intervene and remind them that they will have their opportunity to speak and you would like them to listen whilst the other speaks. In practice, interruptions are quite normal as the listener will probably hear things they don't like and will want to defend themselves. Remind them that they will have an opportunity to discuss the points raised after both have had Individual Time and that listening is not the same as agreeing.

The reason for having Individual Time is to give each an opportunity to present their view of the situation to the other, expressing how it has impacted them. A key factor in the success of the DIY Mediation approach is that it encourages the participant to see the situation from the perspective of the other. Individual Time is a critical element of this.

I am often asked who should go first in the Individual Time. There are a number of ways you can handle this. The option I prefer is to give them the choice. Once you have explained Individual Time simply say:

'So which of you would like to speak first?'

If neither or both of them step forward you could toss a coin, or you could choose one or the other. If choosing, bear in mind you may need to justify your choice if challenged by the other so there should be an impartial reason. If the situation has arisen because one of the participants has made a complaint about the other, a sensible (and justifiable) option would be to ask the one who has complained to speak first.

Individual Time is the participant's opportunity to say what they want. Ideally they will have prepared – hence the importance of outlining at the end of the Individual Meeting that you will be giving them this opportunity to speak. If they are struggling to speak you may need to prompt and assist them through appropriate open questions or ask them to say more about something. Remember though that you should not disclose information you may have picked up from the Individual Meeting as you have committed to keep this confidential. If something is not raised which appears important to you, the participant may have decided not to say it or may have forgotten about it. You can prompt them by asking if there is anything else, but if you want to question why they are not raising something, confidentiality would require you to interrupt the meeting and speak to them privately.

> **KEY POINT**
> After the person has spoken, you should summarise back the
> key points made in their Individual Time. This:
> * ensures that you have picked up the relevant points
> * reinforces the messages for the other participant
> * shows the speaker that you have listened

A good touch is to thank the person who has spoken and also
to thank the person who has listened, acknowledging that it
can be tough to hear things they may not be comfortable with.
You should then offer the second person the opportunity to
have their Individual Time, reminding the first person that
they should listen without interruption. With the second
person suggest they try to refrain from responding to what
they have just heard, instead using their Individual Time to
state what they would have said if they had gone first – ideally
what they have prepared beforehand.

Once the second person has finished and you have
summarised back, again thank them both and you can move
onto the next stage.

Joint Meeting – Discussion Opening

Now they have both heard what the other person has to say
about the situation it is likely they will want to respond. As such
there may be little you need to do to initiate the discussion. If
they do start speaking directly with each other then already you
have achieved something. They are communicating directly,
discussing the issues which have caused them problems. It is
likely this is something they have not been doing and which
has resulted in them sitting in this meeting!

If there is a deathly silence after the Individual Time and
your summary then you need to prompt the discussion. This
could be a general question to them both such as:

'What initial thoughts do either of you have on what you have heard?'

Joint Meeting – Addressing the Trigger Point

At this point in the discussion it is often helpful to focus in on the 'trigger point' i.e. what has happened between the participants which has caused your intervention. It might be an outburst in the office, a direct complaint, a nasty email – whatever caused the ongoing issue between them to get to a point where something had to be done.

> *In our Barb and Sue example, the trigger point was when Barb supplied information to one of Sue's sales team and this resulted in a shouting match.*

By talking through what has occurred in this 'trigger point' interaction you can encourage them to explain why they acted as they did. This helps clarify any miscommunication and false assumptions and moves them towards a mutual understanding of the underlying needs and interests of the other.

> *Barb assumes that Sue has a malicious motive in providing Jeff with the information. She tells Mark in the Individual Meeting that she thinks Barb is 'muscling in on my patch'. This Joint Meeting discussion will test this assumption and Barb can explain why she gave the information. Barb's explanation is that she is only trying to help Sue out.*

Of course, a participant may choose not to believe the reason given but you can challenge this, asking them why they don't believe it and also reflect it back to the other person for them to respond. For example:

> *'Barb, Sue is struggling to fully accept your explanation of why you did what you did. What else can you say that would help in this respect?'*

Another technique you could employ here is to encourage the participants to ask their own questions. They will have answered lots of questions for themselves using assumptions and this is their opportunity to get the answer 'from the horse's mouth'. It might be difficult for them to ask the question so they may need some encouragement, for example:

'Sue, what I'm hearing here is that you are struggling to understand why Barb acted as she did. It might be helpful if you could ask Barb to clarify why she did what she did – is that something you want to ask?'

Clarifying assumptions that have been made is a critical part of the process. As we saw in Section 2 Part 1 – How Conflict Evolves our brain naturally tries to find reasons why someone has acted as they have, and will use the information available to make an assumption. These assumptions are often misinterpretations. Therefore challenging assumptions in this part of the process is vital to shift the perception of the participants as to why the other acted as they did, thereby moving the process forward.

Addressing the trigger point is a useful way to generate helpful discussion. Remember though that in discussing the trigger point you are not trying to decide on the rights and wrongs of whatever happened in that situation. It is simply a means of starting to uncover why they have been behaving towards each other as they have.

Joint Meeting – Dealing with Emotion

I am often asked whether you should stop the meeting if it gets emotional. In my view it is a necessary and helpful part of the process that the emotion felt by the participants (which has been brewing for however long the conflict has been going on) is openly expressed. If you are practising effective

Active Listening you will be noticing and reflecting back to the participants the emotions that you are seeing. Encouraging the description and explanation of the emotion will help each of the participants to understand better the other's perspective.

By encouraging expression of emotion, it is likely that the meeting will become emotional. There could be shouting, crying, gestures or even someone walking out. Provided no-one is abusive or is being purely repetitive then allowing the emotion to be expressed is helpful. Often an emotional outburst is needed to move the process forward. On several occasions when I have been mediating between neighbours, a walkout by one of them has resulted in a positive step forward. It makes sense if you think about it – the walkout is the last resort. If they choose then to come back and continue the discussion it signifies that they are now ready to move on and look forward and invariably this results in a positive discussion after the walkout.

If the emotion becomes too strong and language is getting abusive etc. then you need to intervene and stop the meeting. You could give them a 5-10 minute break and speak to them individually to see where they are at. Emphasise the positive progress that has been made, praise them for the effort put in and keep them focused on reaching a positive outcome. If they are really struggling, consider the options for Dealing with Blockages, covered later in this section.

Joint Meeting – Handling a Demand for an Apology

One of the more common demands in a relationship conflict is that the other person should apologise. This is a classic 'position' statement. The difficulty with apologies is that if one is demanded the other person may simply say no and a dead end is reached. How do we overcome this? As we explored in the Gather Information phase, a 'position' is *what* they are asking for. The critical thing to establish is the underlying need – *why* they are asking it. Avoid therefore getting drawn in to the apology demand. Acknowledge it but ask the person making the demand to explain. What is the specific behaviour that they consider worthy of an apology and why do they feel aggrieved by the behaviour? This will open up the discussion and help understanding of what need is not being met. Very often the apology demand will drop away. Consider this exchange:

Sue – I don't see any point in discussing this until Barb apologises.

Barb – I don't think I've got anything to apologise about.

Mark – Sue, I hear you are looking for an apology. It might be helpful to say a bit more about what in particular you are unhappy about and why it concerns you.

Sue – Well there is simply no excuse for shouting at me when I was just trying to give some feedback.

Mark – So you were trying to offer some information which you hoped would be helpful to Barb and were surprised at the response you got.

Sue – Yes, I was totally taken aback. I thought she had more respect for me than that.

Mark – Barb, Sue is saying she was surprised and disappointed by your reaction to the feedback she was giving.

Barb – I was surprised myself by what she said, it came out of nowhere so that is why I reacted so strongly.

Mark – And on reflection, what do you think of your reaction?

Barb – I can see it probably came across as rude, I was just so surprised.

Mark – Sue, Barb has recognised her response could have been better.

Sue – That's good, I'm not used to being spoken to like that…

Through talking about what happened and why the apology is wanted, Mark has helped Barb to understand that Sue was trying to be helpful and felt surprised and upset by her response. Equally Sue now understands why Barb reacted as she did. It was a surprise and she also acknowledges that it was an overly strong response. So Sue's need (acknowledgement that she was upset when she was trying to be helpful) has been met without getting stuck in the position of whether an apology will be given or not.

Joint Meeting – Summarising Issues

As the discussion progresses, part of your role as Process manager is to formulate in your own mind the critical issues that will need to be addressed. When you feel you have a good idea of what these are, summarise them back to the participants. You should frame these in a forward-focused way as a lead in to looking for solutions. Rather than saying, for example:

'You can't communicate effectively with each other'

reframe it as:

'It would be helpful to you to find ways of improving communication between you both.'

Offer your summary of the issues making it clear that this is what you are hearing from them. It is up to them to accept or add to or amend the list of issues you come up with.

KEY POINT

Once you have made your suggestion check back with them that everything they want to deal with would be covered by the issues you have identified, e.g.:

'If we talked about each of those issues, do you both feel that would cover all the important areas you want to find agreement on?'

One option is to use a flipchart or whiteboard to capture the issues so that everyone can see them as a useful agenda – this is up to you and only do it if you think it would be helpful. You do need to have the specific agreed issues noted so that you can work through them in the next phase.

If you have done your job well – listening and questioning effectively – they should agree on the issues you have proposed. It is really valuable to have something to which they have already agreed so make good use of it. Emphasise it back to them, e.g.:

'Thanks for that, it sounds like you are both agreeing with each other that these are the issues to focus on so that you can find ways to work effectively together.'

KEY POINT

You can safely assume that one of the issues to address will be communication. I haven't come across a single situation where communication has not been an issue – indeed, had the participants been communicating effectively then it is highly unlikely the situation would have deteriorated to the point where your intervention was necessary.

Summary

For the Recognise Issues phase, you have prepared for and opened the Joint Meeting, given each person some Individual Time which you have summarised. During the discussion that follows you have helped them focus on the trigger point, clarifying miscommunication and false assumptions. Once you feel you have sufficient clarity on what the issues are, you have summarised them back and checked that everything will be covered by these issues. You are now ready to progress to the next phase.

Phase 4 – Explore Solutions

Intention: To identify options and optimal solutions to resolve the issues.

This phase will happen primarily in the middle of the Joint Meeting although options and possible solutions could be appearing at any time during the Individual and Joint Meetings. Part of your role as Process manager is to spot and note these when they occur so you can remind the participants of them at the appropriate time.

At this stage of the process you will want to keep them focused on the future. By now you will have discussed the trigger incident and clarified what needs to be resolved, so you have a critical role to keep the process moving forward. You will be supporting the generation of options and solutions and challenging where necessary to ensure optimal outcomes.

Joint Meeting – Brainstorm Issues

Once you have your list of issues you need to pick one to start with. There may be an obvious one, or the participants may start discussing one themselves without prompting. If not, you need to pick an issue.

Here's a useful tip – if there is an issue which, on the surface at least, appears 'easier' to get agreement on then start with this one. The earlier you can get the participants agreeing the more productive the rest of the process will be.

When you have selected an issue, summarise what it is and ask the participants for ideas on how it could be addressed. Encourage them to treat this as a brainstorming session. In other words they should just come up with ideas and not evaluate suggestions at this stage. It is likely you will need to prompt and probe on ideas if they need to clarify them, and use summaries so everyone understands the proposal.

If they are truly stuck for ideas should you help them out? Don't be tempted to jump in too quickly. Remember, the purpose of this process is to help them find their own solutions to the issues they face – you are not there to solve it for them. If they are struggling, prompt them by presenting the issue in a different way, or encourage them to clear the barriers to ideas by taking a 'blank page' approach. For example:

> *'I can see you are finding it difficult to come up with ways to deal with work duplication. If you were to write new job descriptions for your two roles what would be the key responsibilities for each of you?'*

Ultimately, given your experience and knowledge you may be aware of information they don't have, or have ideas on possible solutions which they haven't come up with. If they really need them put these suggestions to them, BUT make it clear they are only suggestions and that they can accept or reject them as they wish. Also, try to make the suggestion a general approach as opposed to specific details. For example:

> *'In similar situations to this I've seen that sometimes people find it helpful to arrange a regular one-to-one meeting with a set agenda. Might an approach like that be something which you would both find helpful?'*

If they want to take this approach, they can decide the details of how it will work – frequency, timing etc. Ideally put more than one idea so at least you are giving options rather than a single solution.

Joint Meeting – Looking for Conciliatory Gestures

In the Explore Solutions phase we might see conciliatory gestures. What are they? These are the moments when one of the participants says something which is helpful to the process. It could be something positive about the other person or conceding something about themselves. Examples would be accepting responsibility for something inappropriate, acknowledging a skill in the other person, or even an apology.

For you as the Process manager these conciliatory gestures are little golden nuggets of opportunity. As such it is important that you spot them and reflect back to make sure they have been heard. For example:

Barb – I find it frustrating when Sue doesn't want to help because she has such a great knowledge of the company.

Mark – Barb, what I'm hearing there is that you really value the experience Sue can bring…

Often these conciliatory gestures go to the heart of the unmet needs of the other person. By emphasising back to them that they have been recognised, or that the other person accepts they have acted inappropriately etc., you are making a very positive contribution to helping them resolve the conflict.

Whilst conciliatory gestures are more likely to come out at this stage of the Joint Meeting – as they should now be focused on the future and how they work together – they could of course crop up at any point during the Joint Meeting. Whenever they occur, spot them and reflect them back. Don't throw away the golden nuggets!

Joint Meeting – Reality Testing

You need to capture the options generated. How you do this is up to you and the participants. You could work with a flip chart, whiteboard, or just rely on your notes. Either way, it is your responsibility to keep track of the ideas proposed so you can review them.

When you have some options for an issue you need to work through them. As each option is discussed, a key role for you is to reality test what is being proposed. Your aim is to help them think through how practical and achievable each suggestion is. You have encouraged them to brainstorm the options so it's likely some of them don't stand up to challenge. Let's look at an example:

One of the issues identified by Barb and Sue is work duplication. An option suggested by Sue is that they delay submission of the marketing report by a day to give them the chance to sit down together to go through it. The reality test needed here is to ask Barb and Sue how that delay would be received by Chris, their manager. You are therefore testing whether the solution proposed has a chance of success, but not by saying 'no that won't work' or 'yes that sounds like a good idea'. Instead you are asking the questions that will enable them to come to their own conclusions as to the feasibility of implementing the solution successfully.

Ultimately if you have information or knowledge which the participants are not aware of and which means a proposed solution won't work you need to feed this in. For instance:

> *Barb and Sue propose that one solution is to recruit an additional team member. Mark knows there is a recruitment freeze. He needs to make them aware of this information so they don't waste time on an option which won't be achievable.*

Remember that when you reality test you are not doing so to give your opinion on a proposed solution. We naturally form our own views on the ideas they come up with but it is important our views do not come through in the questioning. Asking the question with the wrong words or wrong tone could convey your opinion. For instance, rather than asking:

> *'How achievable do you think that might be?'*

you phrase it as:

> *'And you really think that has a chance of working?'*

you are suggesting you don't believe it will work. Unless you have critical additional knowledge, as in the recruitment freeze example above, you must refrain from giving your opinion, and remember, you can betray your opinion in how you say something and the body language you use, not only the words.

Joint Meeting – Identify Mutually Agreeable Solutions for Each Issue

Work through the issues on your agenda, considering all the options identified in the brainstorm. Through discussion identify solutions that work for both participants. The solutions need to be sufficiently detailed to test the practicalities and to leave little room for confusion or misinterpretation. Encourage them therefore to flesh out the proposal.

Let's say that Barb and Sue agree that to improve communication they should have more one-to-one time. Mark would push them to see what that means in practice: 'You are both agreeing that more one-to-one time would be a good way to improve the communication between you. What are your thoughts on how you would go about this?'

Joint Meeting – Agreeing a Mechanism for Dealing with Future Issues

After you have worked through the issues, encourage them to discuss and agree how they want to deal with any future issues or conflicts. Despite all the work you are putting into this resolution process, issues might arise which could spark it off again. It is essential therefore that they agree what will happen if, for example, one of them feels the other has breached whatever agreement they reach. It is a fail-safe mechanism to ensure that future issues do not escalate. Normally this includes how they raise their concern with the other – will they have an informal chat over a coffee, will they drop the other a quick email etc. They need to agree what works for them and you must capture this as a specific point in the final Agreement.

Joint Meeting – Dealing with Blockages

Sometimes during the latter stages of a Joint Meeting the participants may struggle to move the process forward. They may not be able to find options that are acceptable or simply start to run out of ideas. The temptation for you at this point is to 'jump in' and start to solve the problem for them. This risks imposing solutions that are not acceptable to the employees and therefore do not resolve the issues. Resist the temptation and instead try out some of the techniques below to help unblock the process.

A simple mnemonic 'UNBLOCK' provides a tool to help remember the techniques for overcoming blockages.

U nderstand each other's position
N ote agreement
B reak
L eave it to participants
O ffer ideas
C onsequences
K ill it

Figure 16 UNBLOCK tool

• Understand each other's position
At this stage of the process the participants are in effect negotiating with each other. They are therefore representing their own perspective which can lead to difficulties when it appears the perspectives conflict. It is helpful at this point to encourage the participants to see things from the other's perspective using role reversal. You could use questions such as:

'If you were (the other person) how would you respond to what is being suggested?'

or

'In (the other person)'s shoes what wouldn't work for you about that suggestion?'

Another role reversal option is to ask each to summarise what they think the other person's position is and to check back to see if they have understood it. This can highlight misunderstandings or missing key points which could provide an opening to move things forward.

- Note agreement

This is a very useful technique to apply when they can't find agreement on an issue. Go back over what has already been discussed and list out everything they do agree on. This helps give perspective to the one thing they are currently stuck on. It will seem less of an obstacle in the face of what they have already agreed. Also emphasise how well they have done to get to that point and even challenge whether they really want to waste all that effort and hard work over this one point.

- Break

This is the simplest but often the most effective technique – simply take a break. Encourage them to stop thinking about the issue for a short while and they may come back to it with a new perspective. Another option is to switch to a different point and agree to return to the unresolved point later.

- Leave it to the participants

This option is to throw the blockage back to them and make clear it is their problem. It may seem harsh but this technique re-emphasises that you are not there to solve their problem. A simple way to do it might be to say:

'So what would you like to do next?'

or

'It looks like we are stuck on this one so what do you think we should do?'

and then sit back and wait. Remember from Active Listening that Silence is a valuable and much underused technique!

• Offer ideas

The participants should be coming up with their own solutions. However, if they are truly stuck, you may have ideas from previous experience that could be helpful. Float your thoughts but make it absolutely clear that these are ideas only and it is entirely up to them as to whether they want to take them up or not. Be careful as there is a risk they will agree simply because it is what you as HR have suggested – so definitely use this technique with caution.

A less obvious way of using this technique is to construct scenarios. For example:

'What if x did this and y did that, how might that work?'

Even if they don't go down that precise route it might trigger them into an alternative based on that scenario.

• Consequences

This technique challenges the participants to consider the consequences of not reaching agreement. It can be a risky strategy and so should be used carefully. The danger is that one or both of them might realise they are prepared to take the consequences. Usually however this is not the case and encouraging them to think through what would happen helps them realise they need to make an extra effort to resolve the issue.

Your role here is to reality test consequences they may come up with. For instance, if they say:

'I'll take this to an employment tribunal.'

you might want to challenge them on how long this might take, what would be the financial and emotional cost, how might it impact their career.

You can also switch 'Consequences' around, so rather than having them think of the impact of not resolving the conflict, encourage them to think of the consequences of walking out of the meeting with everything agreed. This should push them to a positive mindset which might just be the spur needed to get over the impasse.

- Kill it

This is the nuclear option. Ultimately if participants are not moving forward you have to make it clear to them that you will end the meeting and all the effort that they and you have put in will be lost. The threat alone may be sufficient to get over the final barrier. In the end though there is no point in continuing if there is no way forward and you should end the process if you get to that point.

Finally not every meeting will result in an agreement. The last phase in the **AGREE** model is titled 'Encourage Agreement' and not 'Enforce Agreement', so if encouragement hasn't worked and even the unblocking techniques have had no effect, you always have the option to close the meeting without agreement. Alternative resolution methods can then be considered (see Section 2 Part 1, Figure 3 – the Roadmap for Appropriate Intervention).

Summary

During the Explore Solutions phase you have encouraged the participants to brainstorm options for the issues identified in the previous phase. As Process manager you have helped them by spotting and reflecting Conciliatory Gestures and Reality Testing the ideas proposed. If they find themselves blocked, you have a useful 'UNBLOCK' tool which offers a range of techniques to move beyond the blockage to help them come up with mutually agreeable solutions to their issues. You now want to gain commitment and conclude the process in the final phase.

Phase 5 – Encourage Agreement

Intention: To commit to actions on agreed solutions and implement.

This phase is at the end of the Joint Meeting and pulls together the actions and commitments that have been made during the meeting. It also includes whatever follow up actions are agreed to ensure the Agreement is being effectively implemented. Your role is to maintain the momentum in these late stages and make sure that what they agree is clear, captured appropriately and fully understood.

By this time, late on in the Joint Meeting, it is likely that energy is flagging. The DIY Mediation process can be tiring but ultimate success depends on keeping the momentum going so the Agreement is robust and thorough. Part of your role is to be aware of the participants' energy levels and to encourage them to see the process through. A quick break before committing to the Agreement might be helpful to re-energise.

Joint Meeting – Writing the Agreement

I strongly recommend that you capture any agreements they reach in a written document. Why? So that both the participants and you have an unambiguous record of what has been agreed that can be referred back to if necessary. If the actions agreed are very simple then the participants may not want to have anything more formal than their own notes. If so, you need to make sure your own notes are sufficient to enable you to monitor and follow up as necessary. Far better though is to have a single document that captures the points agreed and which everyone in the meeting signs. This avoids any misunderstanding and simply the act of signing a document helps cement a psychological commitment to keeping to it. Ultimately this is not a legal document. It is a moral commitment which in many ways can be more powerful.

KEY POINT

You should agree the wording and produce the document in the meeting. Don't be tempted to say 'leave this with me and I'll get something to you tomorrow' etc. Everyone should be clear on what is agreed before anyone leaves the room.

It's part of your role to draft the wording. Make a suggestion and see if the words work for them. Remember, it is their agreement, so don't be tempted to add in anything they have not already agreed between themselves. You are simply putting it into wording that makes sense for them both.

How formal you want to make the document is up to you. There is a sample agreement for the Barb and Sue scenario in Appendix Two and you could use this format as a template.

What to include in the Agreement – 5 key points

1. Record the actions agreed and check that they are:

*   FAIR – Being fair means the actions should be balanced and acceptable to all participants. This is not your judgement. If it does not seem fair to you, you can challenge and reality test but ultimately it is their decision. Watch out for one-sided agreements where one participant ends up with all the actions. This is unlikely to be balanced so you need to challenge.

*   SPECIFIC – There is no point in actions which are not clear and could give rise to misinterpretation. Often conflict situations such as these have arisen due to miscommunication so it is critical that the scope for future misunderstanding is minimised. Answering the questions who, what, when and how will ensure actions are specific.

*   ACHIEVEABLE – It is common sense but clearly there is no point in agreeing anything that is not achievable in practice. Reality testing should have dealt with this issue before you reach the Agreement stage.

2. Include a reminder in the Agreement that the meetings, discussion and Agreement are confidential and that all commit to maintaining the confidentiality.

3. Make sure the 'fail-safe mechanism' (see Section 4 – Joint Meeting – Agreeing a Mechanism for Dealing with Future Issues) is included in the Agreement. This will state what the employees will do if they have any future issues with each other. It is a critical part of the

Agreement and what they agree should be specific about what they will do and how they will do it.

4. Include a point in the Agreement regarding how the meeting will be followed up.

5. Ensure the Agreement covers everything that the employees have agreed and check back with them to make sure nothing has been left out. Once you have a draft document, get them to read it and check again if there is anything else they want included.

Figure 17 What to include in the Agreement

Joint Meeting – Agreement Confidentiality

The Agreement belongs to the participants. The confidentiality of the process means that whatever is agreed in the Joint Meeting should not be shared outside of that meeting unless the participants specifically agree. As such the Agreement should not form part of the employees' personnel files or be held somewhere where those not directly involved in the meeting could access it. If someone has an interest in knowing what was agreed – the relevant line manager(s) being the obvious one – then this should be discussed as part of the meeting. The participants need to agree what they will share. They may well be fine to share the whole agreement. If so, this should be noted as part of the Agreement so it is clear to all.

Joint Meeting – Closing

Assuming agreement has been reached and documented as above, you can close the meeting. It is important to end as positively as possible, so thank them for their participation and effort, recognising that it was probably a difficult meeting for them to have. If they have demonstrated that they can communicate effectively with each other during the meeting, reflect this back to them and express your hope and confidence that they can continue to communicate in this way. Finally remind them that you will be following up and will let them know when and how this will happen based on what you have agreed.

Follow Up

With regard to timing you need to allow time between the meeting and the follow up for the participants to put the Agreement into practice. As such a follow up less than two weeks after the meeting will probably not have given them sufficient time. Equally it should not be left too long in case there are issues that need to be addressed. So a follow up within a two-six week range after the Joint Meeting is probably appropriate.

How you do the follow up will depend on what the participants have agreed. It could be that the three of you get together to discuss it jointly, or you may wish to speak to them individually. There are advantages of both approaches but the 'safer' option is to have individual meetings. In this way you can be more confident you are getting the full picture.

I suggest you keep the follow up relatively informal. Rather than going through the Agreement in detail, simply ask them to tell you how things are going. If there is anything that is not going as planned refer them back to the 'fail-safe mechanism' i.e. what they agreed they would do if there was an issue. Encourage them to have the confidence to raise any issues with the other person so they handle it themselves. If things are going better, acknowledge their part in this, congratulate them if you feel it is appropriate and be positive about the future. If there are no major issues there is no need for further follow up unless requested, though obviously you might occasionally check how things are as part of other one-to-one meetings.

If things have truly broken down again, they have used the 'fail-safe mechanism' and it has not worked then you will need to consider other resolution options.

Summary

During the Encourage Agreement phase you have pulled together and captured, ideally in a written document, the agreements that the participants have come to. You have brought the meeting to a close, clarified how and when the follow up will take place and implemented the follow up as agreed. This should conclude the process. Ideally if you have followed the process and applied the necessary skills you will achieve a positive outcome. However even the most skilled and experienced practitioners cannot make people agree if they don't want to. For such cases where the participants won't agree other options are available to you.

Using AGREE for Difficult Conversations

So far we've been focusing on using AGREE as part of DIY Mediation to facilitate others in resolving their conflict. You are acting as the impartial facilitator. However, as an HR professional there are likely to be times when you are involved in a discussion with an employee which has the potential to result in conflict. Typically these times are when you are communicating messages which the other person is likely to find uncomfortable and could elicit an emotional response directed at you. A wide variety of situations could give rise to a 'difficult conversation' but common ones include:

- Tackling a behavioural or performance issue
- Dealing with personal problems
- Delivering bad news such as failure to gain promotion
- Addressing complaints

Given the risk involved in such conversations, how they are conducted is critical. A natural response is to shy away from such conversations, thereby avoiding the issue and potentially adding to the problem. Alternatively having the conversation but using an inappropriate approach could worsen the situation.

Using the AGREE approach combined with the relevant skills enables you to have the difficult conversation in a confident and competent way such that the outcome is positive for both you and employee.

KEY POINT

In a Difficult Conversation the main difference when using AGREE is that you will need to perform a dual role. You are managing the process of the discussion as well as participating in it.

The principles and approach remain similar but with two key differences.

- Preparation – much greater thought is needed when preparing for the meeting
- Meeting process – all phases of the model need to be completed in a single meeting

Difficult Conversations – Preparation

Self-Awareness

Think about how you typically respond in conflict-type situations. What are your 'hot buttons' that could trigger an emotional response? Be ready to deal with emotions, both your own and those of the other person. You need to remain calm and professional so think of strategies you could adopt, such as taking a deep breath, if you feel yourself triggered in the meeting.

Attitude

Set the intention for how you want to be in the meeting. Your approach should be one of curiosity with the aim to listen and explore. You want to respond to what is said, not react. Separate the person from the issue, so your focus is not to blame them but to address the issue.

Perspective

Reflecting on the issue at hand can give new perspectives. Think about assumptions that you may be making. What if those assumptions are not correct? What assumptions might the other person be making and why?

Support

Think about what support is available and what you might need. Do you need to check policies etc.? Do you need to talk to the employee's line manager or your own line manager or any HR colleagues about the approach you intend to take?

Plan

Arrange the meeting at a suitable time and place (e.g. private room, not just before the weekend etc.) and give yourself time to plan. Think in particular about how you are going to open the meeting. If you have to deliver bad news, make sure it is delivered up front. Practise what you are going to say and how you are going to say it.

KEY POINT

If the other person has approached you to say they want to discuss the difficult issue, don't be tempted to address it there and then as you will not have time to prepare. This is particularly important in flare-up situations.

Often there will be a trigger point where the conflict 'erupts'. It could be a belittling comment in a meeting, being shouted at, or perhaps a critical email that is copied to the whole department. Our natural response to an attack of this sort is to defend ourselves, but this can aggravate the situation if we react without thinking it through. The following three strategies will help you avoid this:

1. *If possible, extract yourself from the situation*

Though retaliating might give you some instant satisfaction it will not resolve the situation and could have negative consequences for you. You need time to cool down, so try to remove yourself. In a face-to-face situation, ideally maintain enough control to say something like:

> *'I can see we are both angry; let's discuss this when we've had a chance to calm down'.*

If this is not possible, walking away is better than getting into an argument. If it is an email, close it down, and do something else before you look at it again.

2. *If you can't extract yourself, deflect the attack*

In some situations you may not be able to extract yourself. Taking some deep breaths helps get over the initial flush of anger and you can then use deflective techniques to 'weather the storm'. Phrases such as:

'I see', 'So that's your opinion', 'uh huh', 'I hear that'

can be used to do this. You can also follow it up with a neutrally phrased question e.g.:

'I hear that, but I'm curious as to why you believe my question was insulting?'

Using questions, especially those put across in a calm way, causes the other person to reflect and shift out of the emotional state to a more thinking state. Another method of deflecting is to reflect back the words the person has used:

'So Bob, what you are saying is...'

When they hear their words back they may realise they have been overly aggressive.

3. Demonstrate understanding

It is dangerous to simply say 'I understand' as it can imply agreement or it might inflame the situation if the other person doesn't believe you do understand. Instead, demonstrate understanding through reference back to a specific situation, for example:

'I can appreciate you're angry about not getting the promotion, as I've been in a similar situation when missing out on a job I applied for.'

When preparing for a difficult conversation you need to stand back from the emotion of the situation and take as objective a view as possible. Below are five questions you can ask yourself. Consider each of these and you will be in a good position to have a difficult, but successful, conversation:

1.   How might I or someone else have contributed to the situation?
It is rare that situations are 100% one-sided. Consider what factors may have contributed. For example, if the issue is poor performance, was it made clear by you or the line manager what the expectations were?

2.   What might be a different explanation to the one I have assumed?
We make assumptions to explain why people have acted in a certain way (e.g. she didn't deliver that report on time as she wants to undermine her line manager's position with the director). Challenge yourself to come up with different assumptions (e.g. she didn't deliver that report on time as the director asked her to do something else urgently). This helps create perspective.

3.   What might be underlying issues for the other person?
Often what we see as the surface issue is hiding the real areas that need to be understood. For instance, there could be issues at home which affect how the person behaves at work.

4.   What has been undermined for me in this situation?
If you are already part of the conflict, you may be aware that you have been triggered emotionally e.g. you feel annoyed, upset by an action or behaviour. However, what you probably haven't asked yourself is what important need, interest or value has been undermined for you? For example, if the

employee is rude to you, is it your need for respect that is being undermined? Understanding this will help you explain to the other person why the behaviour is not acceptable.

5. What would be the best outcome for the organisation?
This question focuses on the future and how the situation can best be resolved. It also emphasises that ultimately it is the best interests of the organisation that come first, even if this means it is not the best outcome for you or the other person. For instance, as a Business Partner you really don't get on with one of your client line managers but your own manager wants you to make it work, so you need to find solutions which enable you both to work together.

Difficult Conversations – Meeting Process

Meeting Structure – Difficult Conversation

Open (AGREE Phase 'Act')

- Set out clearly what you are meeting about and how you intend to structure the meeting
- Stress the positive focus – emphasis will be on finding outcomes which improve the situation for both of you going forward
- Establish any ground rules needed – e.g. agree not to interrupt each other, maintain professional approach etc.
- Check they are okay with the approach and if they have any questions before beginning

Present issue (AGREE Phase 'Gather Information')

- Preface by clarifying what you are about to say is your current understanding; you recognise there is another perspective and will listen to their view after you have spoken
- State clearly in neutral language the situation from your perspective. Use the 3 Fs approach
  - FACTS – what happened as you saw it
  - FEELINGS – how it impacted on you
  - FUTURE – what you would like to be different

Listen (AGREE Phase 'Gather Information')

- Give them the opportunity to speak – encourage them to use the 3 Fs approach
- Apply Active Listening skills to ensure you are picking up all key messages from how things are said as well as the words themselves and that you are conveying to them you are listening
- Summarise back at the end to ensure you have understood what the key issues are

---

Discuss (AGREE Phase 'Recognise Issues')

- Clarify where possible any misunderstandings / miscommunications
- Explore each other's perspective, taking a curious approach and avoiding blaming
- Use questioning skills to understand underlying issues
- Use effective communication techniques (see HEAR tool: Section 3 – Assertive Communication)

Way Forward (AGREE Phase 'Explore Solutions')

- Encourage generation of options for how the issues can be addressed
- Narrow down to solutions that work for both of you

Agree (AGREE Phase 'Encourage Agreement')

- Capture and document what is agreed, ensuring actions are specific, measurable and achievable
- Agree how the meeting will be followed up
- Close the meeting

Figure 18 Meeting Structure – Difficult Conversation

Part of your planning should be to consider how best to structure the meeting. This is likely to vary depending on the specific details but the framework above can be used as a guide. It aligns with the phases of the AGREE model detailed earlier in this section. Clearly the key difference to helping others resolve their issue is that you will be covering all phases in a single meeting rather than separate Individual and Joint Meetings.

Dealing with Challenging Behaviour

As these conversations are 'difficult' it is possible you will need to deal with challenging behaviour from the other person which could include being upset and angry / aggressive towards you.

- Remain calm

If you have prepared properly you will have thought through how you will remain calm. The success of the meeting relies on you maintaining a professional approach and keeping the process moving forward in a positive way.

- Don't take it personally

Even if you decide you may have contributed to the situation, don't blame yourself. Often someone else's behaviour is a result of what is going on with them rather than something you have caused. For whatever reason, you may have become the focus of the negative behaviour their personal situation has created. You don't need to take it personally but you do need to address it as the behaviour is causing a business issue.

- Allow venting, respond assertively and be clear on boundaries

If they are angry it will help the other person to vent their anger and 'get it out of their system'. Allow them to do this, showing that you are listening. This should help them calm down. Your response should be calm but assertive. Use the Assertive Communication skills detailed in Section 3.

It is also helpful to establish what is and what is not acceptable in terms of behaviour, thereby setting clear boundaries. For instance, if robust argument is acceptable but shouting is not, state your view clearly and assertively. For example:

> *"When you raise your voice I find it disrespectful and I cannot follow your argument. I recognise you feel strongly but I would like us to agree that we will make our points without shouting."*

- Avoid 'facts' arguments

Different people will have their own perspective on issues and therefore have their own version of the 'facts'. If the versions conflict and there is no way of reconciling them e.g. you both have different recollections of a verbal encounter with no witnesses, there is little point in pursuing the point. The important aspect is the impact that the facts had on both of you and how you will address the issue going forward. Accept therefore you will have different versions and instead focus on the future.

Challenging People

At times we can all be difficult to work with depending on the situation we find ourselves in. Also one person may find someone difficult to work with whereas to someone else there is no problem. As such we should be wary of labelling someone a 'difficult person' to work with. What you should focus on is the specific behaviour of the person that is affecting the relationship. You then need to work with them, having a 'difficult conversation' using AGREE, to address that behaviour and find a way that you can both work together.

However, it can be helpful to think of different 'types' of difficult people as a starting point to understanding and working with them. Below are nine categories describing certain types of difficult people, based on the work of Robert Bramson[9]. Included are some suggestions as to responses that might be most effective with each type. You might find it helpful to consider your difficult person and see if they fit any of these types.

KEY POINT
As with any type of 'pigeon-holing' you need to be very wary of attaching labels to an individual. By all means use the types as a starting point for your own reflection. However, to understand the other person better and to reach a proper resolution of your issues with them you need to have the difficult conversation.

9   *Coping with Difficult People*; Bramson, Robert M, National Seminars Publications, 1981

Table 15 Difficult People

Type	Characteristics	Possible responses
Sherman Tank	• Abusive and intimidating • Attack individual behaviours and personal characteristics • Constant criticism and argument • Believe they are right and care little for others	• Remain calm; wait till they 'run down' • Speak assertively, stating own opinions clearly, don't argue • Maintain eye contact • Be ready to postpone and reconvene later
Sniper	• Front of friendliness which hides backstabbing • Innuendo, teasing and digs • Superior attitude • Avoids confrontation	• Be aware of what is going on • Use questioning to understand what lies behind the attack • Stick with facts • Involve others so not focused on you • Establish communication
Exploder	• Temper tantrums • Outbursts from conversation that may start friendly • Shouting, threatening behaviour • Feels physically or psychologically threatened	• Give them time to wind down • See if they will move with you to a more private area • Use Active Listening to show you take them seriously

Complainer	• Find fault with everything • Moan but do nothing to solve the problem • Expect someone else to do something • Feels powerless and won't engage	• Listen and acknowledge but do not agree or apologise • Summarise / paraphrase, stating facts without comment or argument • Focus on problem solving, asking them where they want this to go • Avoid accusation / defence / further accusation pattern
Clam	• Silent / unresponsive • Refuses to co-operate • Won't open up • Defensive body language – arms folded	• Ask open-ended questions • If respond "I don't know" ask them to take their time or take a guess • Use silence, give time to answer • Present two options and ask them to choose • Pick up on non-verbal signals and feed back what is happening
Ultra-agreeable	• Agree with you but work slowly or won't deliver • Want to be liked, get attention • Over-commit themselves	• Uncover underlying issues that prevent them from taking action • Emphasise valuing their honest opinion • Build rapport – take interest in them • Focus on realistic commitments • Get them to talk about what other commitments they have

Negativist	• Always negative response • Sceptical – 'not worth bothering' attitude • Demotivate others • Feel bitter and not in control of their lives	• Be alert to being 'dragged down' • Focus on similar situations where it has worked before • Remain optimistic but realistic • Don't argue with them • Consider likelihood and impact of worst outcome scenario
Know-it-all	• Think they know everything and make sure others know it • Feel others ideas are inferior / irrelevant • May be condescending / pompous • Can be annoyed by others' knowledge • Need to feel respected	• Be prepared and have all the information you need • Listen carefully, paraphrase back the main points • Don't try to be a counter-expert but present your views as alternatives • Use questions to raise problems but don't confront • Be tentative in disagreement
Staller	• Postpones decisions / won't make a decision • Drags out issues by interjecting different viewpoints • Leaves it to others to progress issues • Perpetual state of information gathering	• Help them be direct by establishing rapport, reassuring them • Explore to understand what is preventing a decision • Give scenarios: "Either this or this will happen. Which is best?" • Help them problem solve, clarify options and prioritise • Support reasonable decisions they offer

In this section we have taken you through the five stages of the AGREE model which give you a step-by-step process to address and resolve the conflict situation. We have also looked at how you can apply the principles of DIY Mediation in the context of a 'difficult conversation'. Combining the AGREE process with the Skills you learned in Section 3 means you are now fully equipped to start practicing DIY Mediation.

Section 5
And Finally…

That's all there is to it! By now you have an idea of what conflict is and you understand the skills and framework to manage it effectively using DIY Mediation. I've packed a lot of information and tools into the book and you may well be wondering how you are going to remember it all. The good news is that you don't have to. I've captured the key points in summary form in Section 6, so if you need a quick refresher you can read that through quickly or refer to specific models, diagrams etc. I've also put a one-page summary of the AGREE model and meeting structures in Appendix Three which you can use as an aide-mémoire.

If you think you've got the basics, try out our free online assessment. It will test your understanding of DIY Mediation and give you a certificate to show you've passed – once you've got the questions right of course! For details of how to access the assessment see Appendix Six.

So now all that's left is for you to try it out. The only way you will consolidate and develop your DIY Mediation skills is by using them. Of course, conflict situations at work don't crop up all the time – fortunately! The skills and framework covered in this book aren't restricted to the workplace though. You may have a difficult situation in your home life, a disagreement with someone in the family or a friend, or maybe you can help two people you know who have fallen out. These are all opportunities for you to try out your skills. Even if there is no obvious conflict situation, the skills we have looked at, Active Listening in particular, can be applied in any situation. Try listening actively when talking to your partner, a work colleague or family member. See how they respond. Do they notice any difference to how you normally are? Do you notice any difference? By practicing the skills and familiarising yourself with the AGREE model you will put yourself in good shape to be able to deal with a conflict situation when it arises. Finally therefore I've pulled together what I consider to be the top five strategies for managing conflict. If you follow all of these then you'll be well on the road from conflict competence to conflict mastery. Good luck!

Five Top Strategies for Conflict Competence

1. *Prevent conflict arising*
This must be the best strategy of all – prevent conflict arising and you won't have to deal with it! Of course, it is easier said than done. By now you will have picked up no doubt that good quality communication lies at the heart of resolving conflict. It is no surprise therefore that the key to preventing conflict arising in the first place is to ensure good communication is taking place. Think of the line managers you would describe as 'good' and those you would describe as 'bad' – I would hazard a guess that the 'good' managers are more effective communicators than the 'bad'. The strategy to adopt therefore is to encourage managers to communicate properly with their teams. Employees who feel they know what is going on and have clear direction and positive feedback will be more engaged and less likely to find themselves in conflict situations. Regular communication is a valuable and effective tool. But do our line managers understand what makes good communication? Often they will know about what to say and how to say it, but do they also recognise the two-way nature of communication? To be effective communicators they also need to be able to listen. Your best way therefore to prevent conflict arising is to ensure your line managers are communicating often and competently.

2. *Spot conflict early*
Despite your best efforts at prevention, conflict will inevitably arise in a workplace situation. So a key strategy for managing it must be to spot it early, giving you an opportunity to nip it in

the bud before it escalates. In Section 2 we looked at Red Flag indicators which enable you and your line managers to receive an early warning that there could be an issue. The natural tendency is to disregard the signals. We'd rather not deal with a potentially difficult situation so we are likely to downplay what we spot or hope that it will go away. Avoidance could be a valid course of action but it should be one that is only taken once the situation has been properly considered. If we do spot the conflict early and take the necessary action – even if we decide that is doing nothing – we stand a much better chance of resolving the conflict as the longer it goes on, the harder it will be to resolve.

3. Intervene competently

You have decided you need to take action and that the action to be taken is for you to intervene. If you have absorbed the principles I've been putting across in this book then you will have the knowledge to make the necessary intervention. The skills to do it effectively will come with practice, so do practise when you can. Follow the process outlined in Section 4 of the book. It is a tried-and-tested process. Follow it, apply the key skills and you will be in a good position to help the participants find a positive outcome. The final element of competent intervention is confidence. If you try to intervene and are not confident when managing the process the participants will quickly lose trust in you. It is a difficult situation for them and they need to know the person helping them resolve it has the belief that they can do it. Therefore be confident – you have the knowledge from learning the process and the skills from practising, so why shouldn't you be confident?

4. Listen more, talk less

The single most common mistake people make when applying DIY Mediation is to do too much talking. Remember that this is a different situation from when you are giving advice and problem solving. It is up to the participants to find solutions and you are facilitating and managing the process. As such you should be doing far more listening than talking. The critical skill here is Active Listening. Learn and practise the elements of the REASSURE model and use them to prompt the participants to do the talking. When you speak it should be to move the process forward, to clarify and explore options and to step in if the process is not being followed, e.g. if one of the participants is interrupting during Individual Time. It is useful to get feedback from the participants after a meeting on how effective you were. Check with them whether they felt you listened sufficiently and whether you spoke too much. It is always worth remembering the old phrase that we were given two ears and one mouth for a reason – more listening, less talking.

5. *Access expert help when needed*

The final key strategy for success is to know when you have reached the limits of your own capability and you need to seek expert help. There is no shame in this. As HR professionals we need to have a wide range of skills so it is natural those skills will not be as well developed as someone who specialises in the area. When you have a situation therefore which you do not feel competent to deal with then turn to a specialist mediator. The difficult question is recognising when you can manage the situation yourself and when you need to seek help. There is no easy answer to this and it will depend largely on your own level of proficiency and confidence. Be careful though – overconfidence could mean you tackle a situation badly and potentially make it worse. Be aware of your company's process and the support options open to you when accessing specialist support. Do you have trained mediators internally? Do you have a regular external supplier? If your company does not have any process set up this is certainly an area to consider. The specialist mediator will need to be briefed by you as to the situation but after that they will manage the process and feed back to you on the outcome to the extent that confidentiality allows.

Section 6
Quick Reference

The Issue

What is Conflict?

Conflict is inevitable in the workplace. Organisations need positive conflict for robust decision-making, creativity and innovation, productive communication and for engagement. How conflict is dealt with determines whether it brings progress or damage. Conflict can become a business problem when disagreements escalate into relationship issues.

Conflict Ingredients

INTERDEPENDENCE	EMOTION
BLAME	BEHAVIOUR

Conflict Causes

Most workplace conflicts occur due to personality clashes or differences in working style. Common to all causes of workplace conflict is the relationship. By addressing the relationship you will go a long way to resolving the conflict.

Conflict Occurs

The issues are the visible symptoms of the conflict but beneath the surface are the needs. Conflict occurs when people's needs are not being met. A DIY Mediation approach helps uncover and address the hidden needs of those involved in the conflict.

Conflict Costs

Conflict costs UK business £33bn per year according to the CBI.

Conflict costs are tangible: employee time, absence cover, legal fees etc., and intangible: decreased engagement and business distraction. It causes negative impact on the business and its people.

Potential Conflict Indicators

Look out for Red Flags shown in significant changes in:

- Activity indicators e.g. attendance, performance, customer complaints
- Behavioural indicators – evasive e.g. withholding information, avoiding personal interaction; and / or invasive e.g. aggression, undermining others

How Conflict Evolves

Conflict spirals round and down:

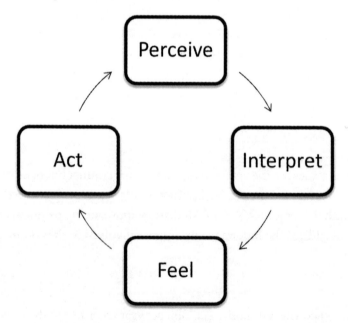

How Conflict Escalates (Glasl)

Stages:

1. *Positions harden*
2. *Debates polarise*
3. *Actions not words*
4. *Images and coalitions*
5. *Loss of face*
6. *Strategies and threats*
7. *Limited destructive blows*
8. *Fragmenting the enemy*
9. *Together into the abyss*

Conflict Styles

Five different styles of conflict response:

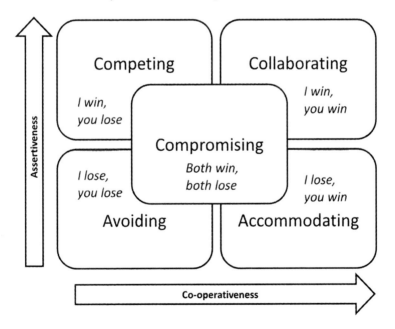

Thomas-Kilmann Conflict Styles

We each have a preferred conflict style. Understanding our style gives greater insight into how we may respond in a conflict situation, enables us to adapt our style and helps us understand how others respond to conflict.

No style is right or wrong but depends on the situation. The nature of the situation will also affect the style we adopt.

Three Conflict Resolution Options

- Power Contest – someone in authority uses their status or power to decide the outcome
- Rights Contest – formal HR processes resolve the conflict
- Interests Reconciliation – using, for example, mediation to resolve the conflict

Roadmap for Appropriate Intervention by HR

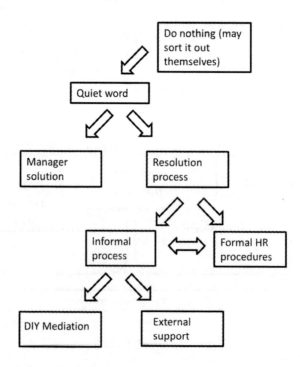

A General Rule of Thumb is:

If it is a clear right / wrong situation then a formal process is better. If the issue is not clear cut then an informal process is preferable.

Deciding on Formal or Informal Process

Formal	Informal
Types of issue	Types of issue
Absolute right / wrong needed	• Communication issues
Clear evidence of injustice	• Personality clashes
Clear disciplinary matter	• Perceived discrimination / harassment
Major power / status differential	• Differences in working style
	• Inappropriate use of power / status
	• Rebuild relationships after formal process
Features	Features
Complaint on record	• Handled confidentially
Structured investigation	• Informal discussions
Laid down timescales	• Timescale flexible
Focus on past / what happened	• Focus on underlying issues / future

DIY Mediation

How DIY Mediation differs from professional workplace mediation.

	DIY Mediation	Professional workplace mediation
Time	Short process – a few hours	Preparation plus whole day for mediation
Skills	Fundamental skills needed	More advanced skills needed
Structure	A clear structure and process flow	Flexible approach within overall framework
Experience	Less experience needed	Professional mediators mediate regularly
Conflict level	For low levels of conflict	More complex cases
Neutrality	Neutrality and impartiality more difficult in own organisation	Professional external mediators are independent

The Skills

Questioning

Open Questions

Why, What, How, Who, Where and When?
Helpful to encourage the participant to open up, to uncover feelings, to probe deeper.

Risk that participant goes off at a tangent. Take care to use 'softening' language with 'why' questions to avoid coming across as intrusive or condemnatory.

Closed Questions

Requiring a 'yes' or 'no' response when it is important to have clarity.

Be careful not to use these questions when you need more than a simple yes / no response.

Hypothetical Questions

A 'what if' type question. Useful to challenge assumptions, promote future focus, prompt thought about alternative scenarios and possibilities, and reality test.

Questioning Pitfalls

Avoid multiple questions – they confuse the person.
Avoid rhetorical questions – they imply an opinion.
Avoid leading questions – they imply an answer in the question.

Planning

Have some questions prepared which you are likely to need. See the tool in Appendix Four – Sample Questions.

Active Listening

Active Listening focuses on all three major elements of communication: body language, voice / tone and words / content. Research found only 7% of a message is conveyed by the words.

Your ability to build rapport and trust through your use of Active Listening skills will help participants relax and open up.

REASSURE – The key skills of Active Listening

Listening is an active process that entails hearing the words, being sensitive to vocal clues, to tone and pitch and inflection, observing movement, taking into account the context and communicating understanding.

R eflecting
E nquiring
A cknowledging
S ummarising
S ilence
U nspoken communication
R ephrasing
E ncouraging

Barriers to Active Listening

* Distractions e.g. external interruptions or heating levels; internal thoughts about the next meeting.
* Rehearsing e.g. thinking about what question to ask next.
* Judging e.g. deciding who is right and who is wrong.
* Identifying e.g. relating the situation back to our experience or feeling sympathy for the participant.
* Problem solving e.g. finding solutions to improve the situation.
* Placating e.g. trying to make a participant feel better.

Assertive Communication

Technique to put across key messages effectively and robustly, especially useful in 'difficult conversations'. A means of modelling good communication skills for the participants.

HEAR Assertive Communication

H appening – state clearly what the problem behaviour is
E ffect – describe how their behaviour has impacted on you
A cknowledge – show you see the situation from their perspective
R equest – state what you would like to happen instead

Impartiality

Remain neutral and do not favour one or other of the participants in how you treat them or view them and their stories.

Why and How to Remain Impartial?

Your role is to facilitate and not judge; impartiality enables development of trust.

Accept you can never be totally impartial; question your assumptions and do not respond to your assumptions or 'hot buttons'.

Assumptions

Assumptions based on things such as appearance, age, manner of speaking, seniority lead to assigning a set of values to the person based on our categorisation. Our natural response is to be more positive towards those people whose values are closest to our own.

Hot Buttons

Be aware of your triggers which prompt you to respond positively or negatively towards somebody.

4 Tips to Help You Remain Impartial

1. *Prepare*
2. *Be aware of judgement potential and consciously avoid it*
3. *Be aware of your own non-verbals*
4. *Seek feedback*

The Process

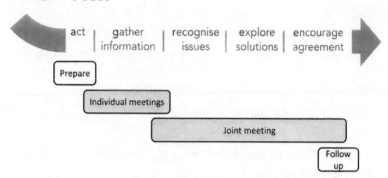

AGREE enables you to work as an impartial facilitator with individuals in disagreement, helping them find their own solutions and reach agreement.

Phase 1 – Act

Intention: To initiate the intervention and prepare yourself and the participants for the process.

Preparation

Decide that an intervention is needed and that you are going to use DIY Mediation. Use the Red Flag Indicators and Roadmap for Appropriate Intervention tools.

Consider timing and setting, ensuring you avoid 'bad' times. Find a private room and make sure you won't be disturbed. Prepare yourself and think through how you will open the meeting, how you will structure it and how you will maintain a positive outlook, impartiality and your own calm.

Meeting Structure – Individual Meeting
– Open
- Purpose and Process
- Informal
- Confidentiality
- Impartiality
- Future Focus

– They tell their story
– Summarise / check understanding
– Advise next steps and Close

Opening the Individual Meeting

Explain at the beginning:

- Purpose and process – support both to resolve issues; will meet them separately and then have a joint meeting
- Informal – not a formal process
- Confidentiality – you will keep what you are told confidential
- Impartiality – not there to judge
- Future focus – focus is on how they can best work together in the future

Use a tone that builds rapport and helps calm them. Establishing trust is critical to your success in helping them resolve the issue. After opening the meeting check with them that they are clear on what you have said and ask if they have any questions.

Phase 2 – Gather Information

Intention: To allow each participant to tell their story, vent feelings and say what they want for the future

Initiate the Information Gathering

- Use a general opening such as 'So tell me about the situation as you see it...'
- *The three Fs* – Encourage speaking about *Facts, Feelings and Future*, i.e. what happened, how they feel about it and what they would like to happen in the future
- *Listen* – Use Active Listening skills to form initial view of key issues / gather sufficient information to decide next step
- *Establish needs and interests* – Understand what needs are not being met. Dig beneath 'what' people say (position) to find out 'why' they are saying it (needs and interests)
- *Summarise* – Check there is nothing else and summarise key points

Closing the Individual Meeting

- Thank them for their time
- Confirm you will get back to them regarding a Joint Meeting as appropriate
- If they express concerns about the Joint Meeting:
  - explore and address concerns
  - clarify the options
  - emphasise the organisation wants the issue resolved
  - Joint Meeting option allows them to agree a solution with the other person

Next Step

After holding both Individual Meetings decide what to do next:

- switch to a different process
- stop the process
- continue to a Joint Meeting; set up the meeting

Phase 3 – Recognise Issues

Intention: To identify the issues that need to be addressed to resolve the conflict

Joint Meeting – Preparation / Opening / Individual Time

Prepare:

- How will you open the meeting?
- What are your possible questions?

> Meeting Structure – Joint Meeting
> – Open
> – Individual Time (no interruption / 3 Fs)
> – Discussion
>   • Trigger Point
>   • Issues
>   • Options
>   • Solutions
> – Write Agreement
> – Agree follow up and Close

Opening meeting:

- Remind about meeting purpose
- Roles and expectations
- Confidentiality
- Meeting structure
- Check for any questions

Individual Time:

- Give each up to 10 minutes each
- Their perspective, covering three Fs

- Don't allow interruptions
- Prompt through open questions if they struggle
- Summarise key points and thank both
- Repeat for second person

Joint Meeting – Discussion / Trigger Point / Emotion / Apologies

- If needed initiate discussion asking for thoughts
- Talk through 'trigger point', asking each to explain why they acted as they did
- Clarify any false assumptions – exploring behaviour not deciding rights and wrongs
- Encourage explanation of the emotion, helps them better understand the perspective of the other
- Emotional outburst can move the process forward. If emotion too strong, intervene and pause the meeting
- Demand for apology is a 'position' statement. Acknowledge and ask them to explain – what behaviour needs apology and why aggrieved

Joint Meeting – Summarising Issues

- Formulate critical issues to be addressed and feed back to participants
- Check all issues identified. One of issues will invariably be communication

Phase 4 – Explore Solutions

Intention: To identify options and optimal solutions to resolve the issues.

Joint Meeting – Brainstorm Issues / Conciliatory Gestures / Reality Testing

- Pick an 'easier' issue and brainstorm. If struggling put suggestion but make clear *only* a suggestion
- Look for conciliatory gestures, where something positive expressed, e.g. acknowledging a skill. Spot and reflect back to emphasise
- Capture options and ideas. Work through each option and reality test if needed – checking how realistic proposed solution is without giving opinion

Joint Meeting – Mutually Agreeable Solutions / Future Issues Mechanism / Dealing with Blockages

- Identify solutions that work for both participants and flesh out proposals
- Need fail-safe mechanism on how to deal with any future issues between them
- Resist 'jumping in' if process not moving forward. Use UNBLOCK techniques
- If encouragement and unblocking techniques have no effect, close and consider alternative resolution methods

U nderstand each other's position
N ote agreement
B reak
L eave it to participants
O ffer ideas
C onsequences
K ill it

Phase 5 – Encourage Agreement

Intention: To commit to actions on agreed solutions and implement.

Joint Meeting – the Agreement / Confidentiality

- Strongly recommended to capture agreements in written document, signed by all. Not legal, but a moral commitment
- Draft the document in the meeting, agreeing wording
- Make sure actions are Fair, Specific and Achievable
- Include confidentiality reminder, fail-safe mechanism and follow up process
- Double check everything is covered
- Agreement and content should not be shared with anyone else, or go on personnel file, unless agreed by participants

Joint Meeting – Closing and Follow Up

- Thank for participation and effort
- Remind them of follow up
- Close the meeting
- Follow up between 2-6 weeks later, keep it informal
- How follow up will depend on what agreed, could all meet together or meet individually
- If issues still exist encourage use of fail-safe mechanism to handle it themselves
- If improved acknowledge their part and be positive about future

Using AGREE for Difficult Conversations

AGREE and the relevant skills can be used to manage a Difficult Conversation i.e. where you are one of the participants as opposed to helping others resolve conflict. The principles and approach remain similar but more preparation is needed and all phases are completed in a single meeting.

Meeting Structure – Difficult Conversation
- Open (AGREE Phase 'Act')
- Present issue (AGREE Phase 'Gather Information')
- Listen (AGREE Phase 'Gather Information')
- Discuss (AGREE Phase 'Recognise Issues')
- Way Forward (AGREE Phase 'Explore Solutions')
- Agree (AGREE Phase 'Encourage Agreement')

Preparation
- *Self-awareness*: consider how you respond in conflict situations and how to remain calm.
- *Attitude:* approach should be curiosity, aiming to listen and explore. Respond rather than react.
- *Perspective:* what assumptions are being made and what alternatives could there be?
- *Support:* who do you need to speak to, what do you need to check?
- *Plan:* don't be drawn in to discussing in heat of moment, extract self from situation and plan; arrange meeting at suitable time and place; plan opening and practice.

Five Questions to Consider
1. How might I or someone else have contributed to the situation?
2. What might be a different explanation to the one I have assumed?
3. What might be underlying issues for the other person?

4. What has been undermined for me in this situation?
5. What would be the best outcome for the organisation?

Dealing with Challenging Behaviour

1. *Remain calm:* need to maintain professional approach and focus on moving forward.
2. *Don't take it personally:* they may be reacting to a personal situation unrelated to you.
3. *Allow venting:* listen, respond calmly and assertively; be clear on what is not acceptable.
4. *Avoid 'facts' arguments:* accept you have different versions and focus instead on future.

Challenging People

We should not label someone as 'difficult' – we can all be difficult to work with at times. Focus instead on the behaviour that is affecting the relationship. Thinking of difficult 'types' can help as a *starting point* to understanding and working with them. Some 'type' suggestions based on the work of Robert Bramson:

Type	Characteristics	Possible responses
Sherman Tank	Abusive and intimidating	Remain calm; speak assertively
Sniper	Friendly front hides backstabbing	Question to explore why
Exploder	Temper tantrums	Give them time to wind down, listen
Complainer	Find fault with everything	Acknowledge, don't agree / apologize
Clam	Silent / unresponsive	Ask open questions, use silence
Ultra-agreeable	Agree with you but won't deliver	Emphasise valuing honest opinion
Negativist	Always negative response	Remain optimistic but realistic
Know-it-all	Think they know everything	Present your views as alternatives
Staller	Postpones / won't make decisions	Explore what is preventing a decision

Five Top Strategies for Conflict Competence

1. Prevent Conflict Arising
2. Spot Conflict Early
3. Intervene
4. Listen More, Talk Less
5. Access expert help when needed

Section 7
Appendices

Appendix One – Barb and Sue Case Study

The Barb and Sue case study that runs through the book is intended to give you an example of DIY Mediation in action. To assist you further the transcript below shows extracts from conversations the HR Manager Mark has with Barb and / or Sue in each of the AGREE phases. The transcript is taken from video demonstrations of the AGREE phases which are available via the www.diymediation.com website (see Appendix Six – Access to Further Resources).

Scenario Outline:

Barb and Sue both work as Sales Support Officers in a telecoms company. They provide admin support for the regional sales team. Sue covers the northern part of the region and Barb the south. The Sales Support Manager, Chris, has asked for the support of Mark, his HR Business Partner, as Barb and Sue are finding it increasingly difficult to work together. Chris has tried speaking to them and encouraged them to sort it out themselves but he is relatively inexperienced himself. After an incident in the office the previous week, where Barb and Sue had a shouting match over provision of information to the sales teams, Chris feels he needs the help of Mark to try to help Barb and Sue find a way to work together. He values both their contributions and individually they are strong performers, but their inability to work together is beginning to affect the team's delivery and reputation. Mark has agreed to run an informal process with Barb and Sue using the DIY Mediation approach.

Act

Mark arranges Individual Meetings with Barb and Sue. His first meeting is with Barb and the meeting opens as follows…

> **MARK**
> *Barb, thanks for having a chat with me this morning. What it's about is that I've been speaking with Chris and he has noticed recently that you and Sue have not been getting along that well. We are concerned about the impact that might be having on both of you. So Chris has asked for my help. What we'd like to do is support you both to work through any issues you are having as none of us want things to escalate and potentially impact badly on the team's work. So I'm going to meet with you and Sue separately and probably then the three of us can get together to find some ways forward. How does that sound?*
>
> **BARB**
> *Mm, well I'd rather you just told her to start including me a bit more.*
>
> **MARK**
> *Well what I'm intending, Barb, is that rather than anyone imposing anything on either of you, I'm going to work with you to help you come up with solutions that work for both of you. To do that I need to remain impartial so I won't be siding with one or the other of you. Also, this is not part of any formal process and anything you tell me I will keep confidential, so you can be open. The focus is very much on making it work going forward rather than deciding the rights and wrongs of what has already happened. I know it is bit of a different approach but I'm confident that by working together we can make the situation better for you, Sue and the good of the team. So how does that sound?*

Gather Information

After meeting Barb, Mark arranges to meet Sue. He opens the meeting in much the same way as in the Individual Meeting with Barb and then carries on…

MARK

So, Sue, that's why we're here. Do you have any questions at this point?

SUE

No, Mark, not at this point.

MARK

It would be helpful then if you can tell me what's been happening from your point of view.

SUE

I don't like her, never have. Nobody likes her. How's anybody meant to work with such a humourless, snobby cow? She never talks, never takes part, never socialises, just sits there hiding behind her computer eating mountains of chocolate which she never shares with the rest of us. Doesn't offer to make anybody a cup of tea, especially not me. She doesn't like me. Never has. Never shown the slightest interest in me or my work. Can't stand the woman. Don't want to work with the woman. Never wanted to work with the woman. She should never have got the job. I'd transfer her out tomorrow. Especially now she's on my patch.

MARK

I'm hearing that you're finding it difficult to work with Barb at the moment. Has anything happened recently with her that you've found particularly difficult?

SUE

Last week's incident.

MARK

Can you tell me more about that?

SUE

Last Friday I was out at lunchtime with the team. We were celebrating with Tony. He'd just won a major account. When I came back to the office later that afternoon I saw a note from Jeff on my desk saying that Barb had helped him with some competitor information. I was livid.

MARK

Why were you angry?

SUE

Jeff is my salesman. He works on my patch... Barb is nothing to do with

Jeff. She's got nothing to say to Jeff. I'm the one who gives Jeff information, not her.

MARK

How did that make you feel?

SUE

Totally undermined. How dare she creep onto my patch! She'll be wanting to take over my entire job soon.

MARK

Is that a real concern?

SUE

What?

MARK

That Barb would take over your job?

SUE

I'd never let that happen. She hasn't got a clue about this job. I'm worth five of her.

MARK

So tell me how you feel undermined by Barb giving Jeff this information.

SUE

Because she's muscling in on my patch.

MARK

Muscling in on your patch?

SUE

I don't want her anywhere near my work.

MARK

Why is that?

SUE

I just don't like her… Claire should have got that job, not her.

MARK

Claire?

SUE

A friend. I don't know why she didn't get it. Barb doesn't deserve it. Claire's much better than her.

MARK

I can see you are disappointed that your friend didn't get the role. How do you think that could be impacting on how you get on with Barb?

SUE

I suppose it could be.

MARK

How would you like things to be with Barb in the future?

SUE

As I'm stuck with her I just want to get on with my work in peace and for her to keep off my patch.

Recognise Issues

After the Individual Meetings with Barb and Sue, Mark decides to proceed with a Joint Meeting. After Mark has opened the meeting, explaining the process and reminding them about confidentiality etc., he gives them both the opportunity to speak in their Individual Time…

MARK

Unless you've got any questions we'll kick things off with Barb. Barb, if you could take a few minutes to talk about what's been happening from your point of view, how you feel about it and how you'd like things to be in the future.

BARB

It's difficult. I don't know what to say.

SUE

Now there's a surprise. Nothing to say!

BARB

There, see. Mark, she just attacks me.

MARK

Sue, this is Barb's turn to talk. You will have your chance to speak soon.

SUE

Sorry, Mark.

MARK

Carry on, Barb. Just tell us in your words how you're finding work at the moment.

BARB

Very hard. Very lonely... Sue scares me. She's so confident. So forceful. She knows everybody in the office and all the sales force and I know hardly anybody. I've been working here for a few months but it's really difficult to get to know people. I know I'm quiet but I'm trying to build my confidence. It's just very difficult with Sue because for some reason...

SUE

Of course, it's my fault.

MARK

Sue, you will have a chance to have your say shortly; please let Barb say what she wants. Carry on, Barb. You're doing well.

BARB

For some reason, Sue doesn't seem to like me. I think I annoy her and she doesn't want to include me in any of the office banter. I'm not invited to drinks on a Friday or any other social events. I find that very upsetting and it has made me feel very lonely at work. Sue never discusses work with me and gives me the cold shoulder. I'm sure we're both producing the same Marketing reports for our sales teams each month. I was only trying to help her out the other week when I gave Jeff that information.

Barb continues her Individual Time after which Mark gives a brief summary and then invites Sue to speak for her Individual Time. After Sue has spoken Mark continues...

MARK

Thank you, Sue, for that and thank you to Barb for listening. In summary you feel that Barb is not joining in with the rest of the office and is isolating herself from the team. You were very irritated that she gave Jeff that information as she knows that Jeff works in the salesforce in the part of the region that you support. You would like Barb to be clear that any information for your sales team should go through you. Have I got that right?

SUE

Yes.

MARK

Okay, thanks both of you for that. I appreciate it can be difficult sometimes to hear things which may be uncomfortable, but it is important you both know how this situation is impacting the other. So have you any thoughts on what you heard there...

The conversation continues with Mark encouraging them to discuss the situation and probing to find out where the issues are. When Mark feels he has identified the issues that need to be addressed he continues...

MARK

Right, so from what you've been saying it sounds like there are a few issues which we need to address. Communication. Work duplication. Socialising. So if we dealt with these would that cover for you the important areas to agree on?

SUE

Sounds right to me.

BARB

Yes.

MARK

Are there any other issues you feel need to be discussed?

BARB

No.

SUE

I don't think so.

MARK

Okay. I think we'll start with the issue of work duplication.

Explore Solutions

MARK
So work duplication. Who would like to go first?
SUE
I will, if that's okay?
BARB
Yes.
SUE
There's no problem with work duplication. It's simple. Barb supports her patch and I support mine.
BARB
Fine.
MARK
So, as you see it, Sue, there's no overlap at all?
Pause.
MARK
Barb, you mentioned a Marketing report?
BARB
Yes. Every month we produce a Marketing report to support the sales force. The report covers Market developments, intelligence, competitor product launches and information from HQ. Anything that can help our sales team make a sale.
SUE
I also put in examples of best practice that I pick up from the sales team which is particularly useful to new sales reps.
BARB
Now that's a good idea.
SUE
I have a very good relationship with them. I have been in the job for ten years.
MARK
Sue, did you notice Barb mentioned your idea was good?

SUE

Yes. Thank you, Barb.

BARB

I know you're good at your job, Sue. I'd like to learn more from you and your experience.

SUE

You want to work closer together?

BARB

Certainly with the Marketing report. I think we could help each other out.

SUE

How?

BARB

I find it hard to produce a full report every month. Could we perhaps discuss sharing the load?

SUE

I like working on my own.

MARK

What are the areas you like working on?

BARB

Well the bit I like is the statistical analysis as that was part of my degree.

SUE

You do?

BARB

Yes. I love numbers.

SUE

Well I prefer people so I enjoy gathering pieces of market intelligence from the salesforce and other contacts which I always include in my report.

MARK

Okay, so Barb, you enjoy doing the numbers and Sue, you prefer discussing the market with the salesforce. What options would there be where you can each focus on the areas you prefer?

BARB

Why are we duplicating effort? Why not focus on our strengths and you produce the market intelligence report and I'll do the statistical analysis?

SUE

I'm so used to working on my own that it hadn't occurred to me that we could split it like that.

BARB

I'm sure we could help each other out.

MARK

So that sounds like something you both think could work so what would you need to do?

SUE

The report is due on the first Monday of every month. We could get together at the beginning of the last week of every month and decide who will provide which information.

MARK

How does that sound, Barb?

BARB

Yes, that sounds great.

MARK

Can I just check that you both think this is a fair split of the work and that one of you will not be doing more than the other?

SUE

The market intelligence gathering is more work as its ongoing and never ends.

BARB

I'm happy to help in other ways as well. I can liaise with Steve at HQ and gather the national information.

SUE

Agreed. He's a pain in the neck.

BARB

I know what you mean.

MARK

Sue, are you quite happy to gather intelligence from Barb's salesforce and Barb, are you happy for Sue to do that?

BARB

I have no problem with that. I think Sue knows them all anyway. One thing I would say is that I need to still be doing that myself anyway as I need to learn to do this myself to support the team. Any information I pick up I'll pass to Sue.

SUE

Barb's right. I know all the salesforce and talk to them already and I agree that she needs to learn how to do this aspect of the job as well.

MARK

Okay, so how will you organise getting the report done together?

BARB

Let's put some dates into the diary as soon as this meeting finishes.

SUE

Yes.

MARK

What happens around holiday time or if one of you is sick?

SUE

We'll have to discuss that further. Shall we come up with an arrangement on this first thing tomorrow?

BARB

Fine by me.

MARK

Well done. That's one thing agreed already.

Encourage Agreement

MARK

Let's review what you've said already. Please say if you disagree or would like to change the wording. What I've got is as follows. First point. Sue and Barb, you agree to work together to produce the monthly Marketing report and will meet in the last week of each month to discuss who will complete which part of the report. Sue and Barb also agree to meet tomorrow to discuss the production of the report if one of you is on holiday or ill at the relevant time.

SUE

Fine with me.

BARB

Me too.

MARK

Secondly. Sue and Barb to meet at nine o'clock on a Monday morning to discuss any potential work duplication that can be avoided in the coming week and how you may help one another out.

BARB

Can I change something?

MARK

What would you like to change?

BARB

Sue, if it's alright with you can we make it 8.30 as our team meeting is at 9.15 on a Monday and I need time to prepare the room.

SUE

I need it to be nine, Barb. 8.30 is too early as I take my grandchildren into school before coming into work.

BARB

Oh.

Pause.

MARK

Can either of you think of any alternatives?

SUE

There's no point having the meeting any other time. It has to be first thing on a Monday.

BARB

Yes.

MARK

How long will you need for the meeting?

SUE

Only ten to fifteen minutes.

BARB

Yes we'll just need a catch-up to check we're not going to be working on the same thing that week.

MARK

So your meeting will only be ten or fifteen minutes?

BARB

Yes. Sue, can you make it into the office for 8.45 or 8.50? As long as I have ten minutes to prepare the room for the team meeting at 9.15 that will be fine.

SUE

I'm normally in a few minutes before 8.45 so as long as I have to time to make a coffee that time works for me.

BARB

Great. I'll have your coffee ready.

MARK

That's good. Sue and Barb you agree to meet at eight forty-five on a Monday morning to discuss any potential work duplication that can be avoided in the coming week and how you may help one another out. Is that okay?

BARB

Yes.

SUE

Yes.

MARK

Now one thing I'd also like you to agree is how, in the future, you would deal with the type of situation that happened last week with Jeff.

SUE

You mean if Barb gave information to one of my sales team again?

MARK

That, or any other situation where you have a disagreement.

SUE

As I said I did overact on that issue because I didn't understand you, Barb, and to be honest I was cross that my friend Claire hadn't got the job.

BARB

I never knew about Claire and I want to reassure you that I'm not trying to muscle in on your patch. I'm trying hard to get to grips with my own.

SUE

I don't think this will be an issue in the future and if it is I suggest we agree to talk about it privately.

BARB

Sounds good to me.

MARK

Okay, I'll add that in as well. Well done. You've both worked very hard today and come to a number of agreements. Let's all keep an eye on things and I'll check back with you in the next couple of weeks to see how things are going. Thank you.

Appendix Two – Barb and Sue Agreement

AGREEMENT

Date:	1st April 2015
Employees Present:	Barb Harding
	Sue Sweetman
HR Manager:	Mark Knowles

The Employees named above have discussed their issues with the abovenamed HR manager and have agreed as follows:

Communication

- Sue and Barb both recognise that to do their jobs effectively they each need to be informed about significant work developments and agree to share any key work-related information that they become aware of.
- When Sue and Barb email any member of the others Sales Team they agree to cc the other into the email.
- Sue and Barb agree that when they speak with each other they will do so in a respectful, professional and mature way.

Work Duplication

- Sue and Barb agree to work together to produce the monthly Marketing report and will meet in the last week of each month to discuss who will complete which part of the report.
- Sue and Barb both agree to meet tomorrow 2nd April 2015 to discuss the production of the report if one of them is on holiday or is ill at the relevant time.
- Sue and Barb agree to meet weekly at 8:45 on Monday to

discuss any potential work duplication that can be avoided in the coming week and how they may help one another out.

- Sue and Barb both agree to have a private conversation if either of them feel the other is encroaching on their work area.

Socialising

- Sue and Barb agree that if either organises an office social event they will invite the other.

Future Disagreement

- Sue and Barb both agree that if there is significant disagreement between them which could cause team disruption, they will request an urgent meeting with the other and seek to resolve the disagreement in the best interests of the team.

The Employees and the HR Manager agree to keep the contents of this Agreement confidential.

Signed

Barb Harding
Sue Sweetman
Mark Knowles

Appendix Three – AGREE Model Summary

act | gather information | recognise issues | explore solutions | encourage agreement

Prepare → Individual meetings → Joint meeting → Follow up

agree model

Enables you to work as an impartial facilitator with the individuals in disagreement, helping them find their own solutions and reach agreement.

act

To initiate the intervention and prepare self and participants for the process.

- Decide on intervention
- Agree time / place
- Prepare (calm, positive, non-judgemental)

Individual Meeting Structure
- Open
  - Purpose and Process
  - Informal
  - Confidentiality
  - Impartiality
  - Future Focus
- Their Story
- Summarise / check understanding

gather information

To allow each participant to tell their story, vent feelings and say what they want for the future.

- Facts, Feelings, Future
- Use Active Listening skills
- Summarise back and check there is nothing else
- Arrange joint meeting

Individual Meeting Structure
- Open
  - Purpose and Process
  - Informal
  - Confidentiality
  - Impartiality
  - Future Focus
- Their Story
- Summarise / check understanding

recognise issues

To identify the issues that need to be addressed to resolve the conflict.

- Your role: process management
- Remember REASSURE
- Agree issues to address
  - Identify from Individual Time and Discussion
  - Confirm with participants

Joint Meeting Structure
- Open
  - Individual Time (no interruption / 3 F's)
  - Discussion – issues, options, solutions
  - Agree and Close

explore solutions

To identify options and optimal solutions to resolve the issues.

- Work through agreed issues
- Generate options
- Reality Testing
- Seek mutually agreeable solutions

Joint Meeting Structure
- Open
  - Individual Time (no interruption / 3 F's)
  - Discussion – issues, options, solutions
  - Agree and Close

encourage agreement

To commit to actions on agreed solutions and implement.

- Seek agreement – written preferably
- Ensure all issues covered
- Mechanism for dealing with conflict if arises again
- Fair, specific, achievable
- Follow up with each

Joint Meeting Structure
- Open
  - Individual Time (no interruption / 3 F's)
  - Discussion – issues, options, solutions
  - Agree and Close

Appendix Four – Sample Questions

It is strongly recommended you develop your own style and questions that you feel comfortable with when using DIY Mediation. This tool is intended to provide a starting point, to help you particularly when you are beginning the DIY Mediation approach. The questions are organised into the phases of the AGREE model where they are most likely to be helpful, but many can be used in more than one of the model phases. No questions are included for the Act phase as Act is about your preparation and opening the meeting so questions only begin in Gather Information.

Gather Information	Kicking things off	• How have things been at work for you recently? (very general) • So talk me through what's been happening between you and X? (more specific)
	Getting to feelings	• How did you feel when…? • Help me understand your feelings about…?
	Probing deeper	• Tell me more about…? • What happened next? • What was your reaction to…?
	Seeking clarification	• Am I understanding you correctly when I say…? • I hear you saying… Is that accurate?
	Challenging	• Why do you think you acted in that way? • Why do you think X may have responded as they did?
	Understanding needs and interests	• Why was that important to you? • Why do you think that affected you so much? • What do you think was being undermined for you in this situation?
	Future Focus	• How would you like things to be in the future? • What changes would you like to see?
	Wrapping up	• It sounds like these are the important issues to you…? • Is there anything else you would like to tell me?

Recognise Issues	Opening Individual Time in the Joint Meeting	• So, X, perhaps you'd like to start. Could you explain to Y your view of the situation, how you feel about it and what you would like to happen going forward? • Would one of you like to start by explaining to the other how you see what has been going on, the affect it has had on you and how you see the future?
	After Individual Time	• What did you think X about the points made by Y? • X, how did you feel after Y's comments?
	Agreeing issues to address	• What do you feel are the issues that we need to address? • From what you've said it sounds to me like we need to look at... would you both agree? What other areas should we cover? • What do you think needs to be resolved?
Explore Solutions	Options generation	• What ideas have you got on how you can address this issue? • What alternatives might there be?
	Challenge / Reality Test	• What do you think the practical implications / consequences of that would be? • How in practice would you make that happen? • What barriers do you see in making that solution work?
Encourage Agreement	Overcoming negativity	• What happens if you are not able to reach agreement today? • What are the possible outcomes if you decide to follow a grievance process? • You've made such great progress today towards resolving this issue; what's the final thing needed so we can all walk away with this matter sorted?

Appendix Five –
Simple Conflict Styles Questionnaire

This questionnaire is intended as a simplistic tool to give an indication of your likely natural conflict style (see Section Two – Five Conflict Styles). Read the scenario in each question and pick the response which describes how you would *naturally* respond to the situation described.

1. *You have an urgent report to complete by the end of the day. Your manager calls you into his office to discuss the impending office move for which you had worked hard at producing an in-depth plan. He tells you he is not happy about your desk layout proposal. Do you:*

A. Ask him to email you what he's not happy about and you can make some minor tweaks but nothing major.
B. Tell him you know from all the work you've done it's a really good proposal and to stick with it.
C. Say you will make the changes he wants but can it wait till the morning.
D. Say you will sit down to discuss the plan with him to explain why you did it that way and to hear from him what his concerns are.
E. Tell him you can't meet at the moment because of the report deadline and then hope he won't mention it again.

2. *Your team has to select one of the team to negotiate with IT for resources to upgrade the online performance management system. You know it will be difficult as other departments have important projects for which they also need IT resources. Do you pick someone who:*

A. Would make sure most of what your team wanted was achieved but without upsetting other departments.

B. Is strongly in favour of your project so will argue robustly for it.

C. Would recognize the value of maintaining good relationships with the other departments and adjust your team's requirements accordingly.

D. Can argue the merits of your project and would listen to the cases put forward by the other teams and work with them to problem-solve jointly.

E. Would present the case clearly, would refrain from getting into difficult debates and would rely on a sensible decision being made.

3. *You and a colleague have been tasked by your director with drafting a new policy. You are in agreement on most of the points in the policy but there is one that is a real sticking point. The deadline is approaching and it still hasn't been resolved. Do you:*

A. Look again at what you want and consider what you might be flexible on to reach agreement.

B. Review what your colleague's argument is and prepare how you can respond to each of the points they might make and think how they might argue against your case so you can defend it.

C. Think about the consequences of digging your heels in and how it might affect your relationship with your colleague and how you are both perceived by your director.

D. Suggest to your colleague that you book out a couple of hours to go through the point again, stressing that you should be able to find a win-win solution.

E. Recognise that there is no point in spending more time on it and leave it to the director to decide on the better solution.

4. *One of your closest colleagues who you also count as a friend has lost the HR textbook you lent her for her studies. She had apologised*

and you said you didn't mind and she said she thought so as you didn't need it anymore anyway. This has annoyed you as you did use the book to refer to and it was important to you. Do you:

A. Tell her it doesn't matter too much and she can buy you a drink instead when you next go out.
B. Think, 'I'm not having this' and you tell her she shouldn't assume it isn't important and you want her to replace it.
C. Recognise you were getting upset unnecessarily. It's far more important that you maintain your friendship.
D. Ask to meet up for a drink with her and explain to her that you are upset and ask her to say what she thinks about it.
E. Be cross with her but don't say anything and replace it yourself.

5. *Your manager has sent you on a personal development course and the trainer has given you five one-liners which represent different life philosophies. You have to choose the one which fits you best. Which would it be:*

A. You win some you lose some.
B. Life is for winning.
C. Often it is best to turn the other cheek.
D. Everyone can contribute, no matter who they are.
E. If it's not worth it, move on.

Results

The responses align to the following conflict styles:

A – Compromising
B – Competing
C – Accommodating
D – Collaborating
E – Avoiding

Look at your responses and see which letter, A, B, C, D or E occurs most. So if you have, for example, 3 As, 1 C and 1 D your natural style is Compromising. Dominance of one letter indicates a strong natural style, e.g. all Bs would indicate a strong Competing style. If your answers are evenly spread, say one of each letter or just two of one letter, it indicates you don't have a strong natural style and can operate from different style perspectives.

For a more comprehensive evaluation of your conflict style you should complete the full Thomas-Kilmann Instrument which can be bought online.

Appendix Six – Access to Further Resources

TEST YOUR KNOWLEDGE OF DIY MEDIATION AND DOWNLOAD PERSONALISED CERTIFICATE

If you would like to put your DIY Mediation knowledge to the test you can take our online assessment. Simply go to www.diymediation.com, enter your details and take our free assessment. Answer the questions correctly and you can print off your own personalised DIY Mediation certificate.

ADDITIONAL DIY MEDIATION RESOURCES

Free Mediation Infobites

You can sign up for our free online Mediation Infobites. These are a series of bite-sized videos specifically developed for HR professionals to help build your knowledge about mediation and conflict resolution. Find the Mediation Infobites at www.mediation4.co.uk.

Premium Tools and Resources for DIY Mediation

All the information you need to practise DIY Mediation is contained in this book but we've produced some additional resources which are designed to make DIY Mediation even easier for you to use:

- *Video demonstrations of AGREE model phases using the Barb and Sue scenario*
  Appendix One gives the transcript of the Barb and Sue scenario that runs through this book. It's sometimes difficult to visualise how this looks in reality so we've produced five short videos from this transcript so you can see DIY Mediation in action.

- *Downloadable quick reference guide to AGREE and key tools*
  In a DIY Mediation meeting it can be handy to have an aide-mémoire of the AGREE model and the key tools used in DIY Mediation. This downloadable quick reference guide gives you the essence of what you need to know on one double-sided sheet of A4.
- *Downloadable notes templates for Individual and Joint Meetings*
  These two template forms, one for Individual Meetings and one for Joint Meetings, enable you to capture the key points under relevant headings and will give you a valuable record of the meetings held. They also include helpful reminders such as meeting structures.
- *Downloadable agreement template*
  The agreement the participants come to at the end of the Joint Meeting can be in whatever format works for you all. If you'd like a template to work from, download this tool which is a Word-based Agreement template to use as a starting point.
- *Sample Question Sets*
  In Appendix Four I've given you a selection of sample questions you can use in DIY Mediation. This tool gives you even more questions – of course it is best if you can come up with your own but these are intended to give you a helping hand.
- *Excel-based Cost of Conflict Calculator App*
  In Section 2 I talk about the Cost of Conflict and give the example of how much the Barb and Sue scenario could cost the organisation. To help you calculate the cost of conflict in your own organisation you can download and use this Excel-based app which will take you through all the possible costs involved in a typical workplace conflict.

All these valuable tools are available to you to use whenever you like for a low one-off purchase. For details visit the website at www.diymediation.com.

DIY Mediation Online Learning Series

This book teaches you all you need to know about DIY Mediation but I appreciate that a book is not best suited to everyone's learning style. If you have friends or colleagues who would like to learn DIY Mediation but who would rather have an online option, they can benefit from our Learning Series. Through this series of short videos they can learn the four key skills and the AGREE model process. For details visit the website at www.diymediation.com.